interior style

How to use color
throughout your home

written by
Lesley Riva

Benjamin Moore®
Paints

For information, write to Benjamin Moore & Co.,

Attn: Communications Department

51 Chestnut Ridge Road, Montvale, NJ 07645.

www.benjaminmoore.com

Interior style / written by Lesley Riva.– 1st ed.

    p. cm.

ISBN 0-06-075602-0 (pbk. with flaps)

1. Color in interior decoration. I. Riva, Lesley.

NK2115.5.C6I567 2004

747'.94–dc22   2004007647

ISBN 0-0607-5602-0

First U.S. Edition

04 05 06 TOP 10 9 8 7 6 5 4 3 2 1

PRODUCED BY SMALLWOOD & STEWART, INC., NEW YORK CITY

Printed in China

Note: All colors identified in the photographs used throughout
this book are from the Benjamin Moore & Co. Color System. It is
always recommended that you use Benjamin Moore® Color System
chips or consult your Benjamin Moore® retailer when making your
selections. Color names and numbers used throughout this book
refer to either Benjamin Moore® Color Preview® Collection or
Benjamin Moore Classic Color Collection™

contents

Introduction 11

The power of color 12
How color affects our moods and shapes our perception of the rooms around us

The power of light 14
The impact of light on color: Daylight • Artificial light • Night light • Seasonal light • Exposures

Painting a room 16
Pulling a room together with paint: Doors • Baseboards • Floors • Ceilings • Walls • Windows • Trim

Finding your palette 18
The first steps to finding the right color palette for your home.

The color wheel 22
Color terms defined • Refining your preferences color by color and finding the paint to match

Color inspirations 40
From traditional to ultramodern, townhouses to country homes, subdued to saturated colors: Inspirational projects by leading designers.

Practical matters 130
Getting down to the business of painting: Before you begin • Preparing surfaces • Priming • Treating walls, doors, windows, floors, trim • Cleaning up • Storing paint • Types of paint • Paint finishes • Paint safety and disposal

Photography Credits 142

Acknowledgments 142

Designer Directory 143

Introduction

WHEN IT COMES TO INTERIORS, COLOR is downright magical in its power to transform. It warms a chilly room, adds sparkle and interest to a plain space, cools and refreshes a tired corner. It's the most potent instrument we have to shape and personalize our environment. And paint is its natural medium.

Benjamin Moore Interior Style offers practical advice and inspiration on the use of color and paint in your home, taking the guesswork—and the fear—out of both. Sections on the basics of color explore its ability to shape space and influence emotion; its interaction with light; and its powerful effect on perception. There's a quick look at the "science" and language of color, and advice on how to build your personal color palette.

Once you've determined your color preferences, we show you how to find paint colors to match by narrowing your choices in each color family. For those of you eager to get down to work, there's a section of step-by-step instructions and tips to make your painting easier and more successful.

But for all the guidelines and practical information, choosing colors—and the paints that bring them to life—is a matter of personal expression, not scientific theory. To that end, the heart of the book is a guided tour of designer homes, each with its own unique style and palette. These gorgeous interiors will stimulate the imagination, delight the eye, and perhaps provide ideas for your own decorating projects.

The world of color, it turns out, is a subjective one, and the best color schemes are simply the ones that make you happy to be home.

Note: Printed colors can only approximate the color of a coated paint chip. Use actual Benjamin Moore® Color System chips when making a color selection.

The power of color

Color is central to our daily experience. It can change our perception of the space around us, turning it cool or energetic, spacious or cozy. It can affect us emotionally as well, making us feel relaxed, refreshed, excited, reflective. Though its powers are subjective, speaking to each one of us differently, we can make some general observations about how color works.

• **Setting a mood.** Studies have long shown that color has a direct, physical effect on us. Red stimulates appetite; blue lowers blood pressure and slows heart rate; green boosts concentration. The emotional effects of color can be just as measurable: The glow of red walls may feel as warm as an embrace; a breezy room done in ocean blue as refreshing as a summer swim.

• **Shaping space.** The old maxim says that warm colors advance while cool colors recede, but our perception of space actually has more to do with the intensity of color than with the hue itself. Dark or intense colors pull the walls closer; pale, soft colors push them back. A long, narrow room, for example, can be visually reproportioned by painting the two end walls a darker color, drawing them in toward the middle. Conversely, painting a low ceiling a light shade will give it an extra lift. Our sense of space is also affected by contrast. Black

WALLS: Odessa Pink, HC-59.

ABOVE: Interior designed by C&J Katz Studio.
WALLS: Clinton Brown, HC-67; TRIM: White.
BELOW: Stratton Blue, HC-142.

furniture against bold blue walls with bright white trim will make a room feel smaller, as the eye is drawn to its angles and perimeters. A low-contrast scheme—wood tones against honey walls with creamy trim—creates a borderless envelope of space, so the room feels larger. A small room painted entirely in one pale shade may feel largest of all, as walls and ceiling bleed into one another and disappear.

Contrast can also break up the boxy, cramped feel of a square room. Painting one wall (usually directly opposite the entrance) a dramatic accent shade weights the space at one end and adds visual interest.

• Shifting the focus. Color can help divert attention from almost any architectural flaw. Strong shades can serve as a decoy—a bright splash of scarlet at one end of the room can pull the focus away from an ill-proportioned entry at the other. Visible plumbing or ducts can be camouflaged by painting them the same color as the walls, or played up as funky industrial detail with a bright, contrasting coat. An off-center nondescript brick fireplace can be re-created as a focal point by painting the brick a brilliant shade; a minuscule powder room can be clothed in such a riot of color that the eye never notices the tiny dimensions.

The power of light

WALLS: Chocolate Sundae, 2113-10.

Light is the essence of color. Without it, we see no color at all. It's only natural, then, that color changes radically with the type and amount of light. The same shade of pink may look pastel in the fluorescent light of a paint store, pallid in the bright sun of the parking lot, and overpowering on the walls of your bedroom.

• **Daylight** is the truest, most balanced light, though of course it shifts throughout the day, from cool morning light to strong noonday sun to slanting red afternoon rays. The standard advice is that cool colors look best by day, while warm colors come into their own by lamplight at night. In practice, this might mean reserving cool greens or violet-tinged blues for a breakfast room warmed by morning sun, or other areas used mostly by day, such as sunrooms or children's playrooms.

• **Artificial light** varies tremendously. Fluorescent lighting, often used in offices and work areas, lacks the warm colors of the spectrum, so it tends to make warm shades appear dull and flat. Look for "daylight-balanced" bulbs to avoid this effect. Most incandescent bulbs emit a warm yellow light, so cool colors can look gray and washed out. Halogen bulbs produce a clear, white light, close to daylight, which tends to intensify colors.

• Night light. Rooms used mostly at night—dining rooms and dens—are the classic choices for warm color. Incandescent bulbs and candles tend to cast a yellow light, which draws out the warm tones of ochers, rose pinks, and terra-cottas, so they flatter faces and emit a welcoming glow.

• Seasonal light. Summer light is stronger, warmer, yellower than winter light and is often filtered through the green foliage of trees and surrounding landscaping. In many climates, winter light can be gray, flat, and stark. Seasonality should be considered in choosing colors, particularly in vacation homes such as ski cabins and beach houses.

• Exposure. It's oft repeated, and often true: Cool colors work best in south-facing rooms, warm colors in north-facing rooms. A room with southern exposure can feel uncomfortably hot when warm colors are bathed in strong afternoon sun, while the cool gray light of a room with northern exposure feels more welcoming when it meets a warmer shade on the walls.

WALLS: Chelsea Gray, HC-168; **TRIM:** White.

Breaking a room down into its parts can help determine how best to pull it together. Start by choosing the wall color, then decide what you want to highlight—decorative moldings, an attractive view, a collection of art. In general, limit yourself to no more than three colors—walls, trim, and ceiling—with perhaps a fourth reserved for special accents.

Painting a room

doors Usually done in the trim color. A glossy finish, such as pearl, satin, or semigloss, allows for easy cleanup. Highlight doors of special interest with color; paint multiple doors in a room the wall color to prevent choppiness. Remember that the reverse side of the door will be fully visible in the room into which it opens, so colors should be harmonious.

base moldings Usually done in white, or in the same shade as the trim, in a low-luster or semigloss for easy cleanup. Paint narrow moldings the same color as the wall to blend in. Dark or black baseboards can add an unusual shot of sophistication.

floors Wood floors are usually stained or painted with a durable floor enamel. Dark floors ground a room; light floors make furnishings appear to float. Using only one color throughout a house promotes visual flow from room to room.

ceilings Traditionally painted a flat white, though some designers prefer a warm off-white to avoid casting a chilly pall. In a large room, darker colors pull the ceiling lower, making the space cozier; in a small room, pale colors push it higher. A semigloss finish can add a luminous glow, but it requires a smooth surface and a skilled painter.

walls Choose the wall color first, as the anchor shade for the room. Washable matte or eggshell finishes are the most popular—they're nonreflective and hide surface imperfections. A semigloss or satin finish can add sparkle, but the reflective quality also emphasizes any surface irregularities, and the shiny finish can feel cold.

windows Casings are generally painted in the color of the trim; a darker shade tends to pull the eye toward the view. Sashes are sometimes picked out in a second color.

trim Woodwork and trim are usually picked out in a color that contrasts with the walls. High-gloss, semigloss, and satin finishes make a textural contrast, and stand up to washing. Darker trim against light walls focuses attention on handsome woodwork, while traditional light trim works well with all colors. Trim can also be painted out in the wall color; for a seamless look—a good option in small rooms or those with modest moldings not worth emphasizing.

Finding your palette

Choosing colors can be one of the most satisfying parts of designing a home—or the most overwhelming. Here are a few easy steps to help focus your tastes and ideas.

• What's in your closet?
The prevailing shades lined up in your closet—or the absence of them—will tell you a lot about what colors you're comfortable with. If you don't like to wear bright colors, you probably don't want to live with them. On the other hand, you may have seen enough khaki to last a lifetime and are ready for a sea change.

• What style is your home?
Ornate Victorians, streamlined contemporaries, humble bungalows—architectural style can help determine interior as well as exterior color choices. For a period house, examine the historic palettes offered by paint dealers, or research interior colors at a local historical society. If you live in a clean-lined contemporary, having only pure whites may feel right. Just remember that the house's style doesn't have to dictate in the end. If you love fresh-feeling neutrals or brooding, complex shades, adapt the style to your own color preferences.

ABOVE: Interior designed by Jamie Drake.
WALLS AND TRIM: Summer Plum, 2074-20.

BELOW: Interior designed by Louis Aubert.
WALLS: Ice Formations, 973; TRIM: White.

• Where do you live? Take your color cues from the environment. A country retreat or seaside home may cry out to be connected to the outdoors—the gray-blues of the beach, the reds and ochers of the Southwest, the browns and greens of the mountains. A big-city apartment may lend itself to brighter, saturated jewel tones because there is no natural world outside the window, or it may beg for soothing neutrals in reaction to the bustle on the street.

• What inspires you? A deep green from a handsome vase, a faded rose from an antique poster—whatever the shade, and whatever its provenance, colors can often be computer matched (if they don't exist already). Just take the object to your local paint retailer; the minimum requirement for computer matching is a sample about the size of a quarter.

• What do you already have? Your home is filled with color before you pick up a paintbrush, from flooring and cabinetry to fabrics and furnishings. A favorite upholstery fabric can be the starting point for an entire color palette: The most dominant color (often the background shade) might work as the wall color; a second color could become the trim; and a third, less dominant tone could be used for accents.

What's your floor plan? Colors are greatly affected by the layout and flow of your home. In general, a space with long sight lines, where several rooms are visible at the same time, will benefit from a coordinated, coherent color palette.

Choosing one color for all the trim throughout your house will tie diverse spaces together, even if you use different shades on the walls of each room. Stand-alone rooms—bedrooms, baths, studies—can usually be handled independently, because of the clear visual break provided by doors. Another trick to tie rooms together with color is to reverse wall and trim shades in adjacent rooms; the trim in one room becomes the wall color in the next.

In an open progression of rooms where walls are kept neutral, ceilings can be the place for sampling different shades. In a reversal of the traditional pattern, wall color can remain constant, while ceilings vary from room to room. In a small room, continuing the wall color up and over the ceiling enlarges the space by eliminating visual breaks.

What's your hurry? Once you've chosen your colors, don't rush to start work. The first, most crucial step is to try out your selections.

No color chip can accurately reproduce how a color will look in your home. The small size of the chip, the fluorescent

Above: **WALLS**: Philadelphia Cream, HC-30;
TRIM: Linen White; Antique White.
Below: **WALLS**: Sunny Afternoon, 356;
TRIM: White.

light of the store, the different surroundings—all guarantee that the shade in your hand will look quite different on the wall. That's why experts tell you to test colors on site.

For the minimal cost of a quart of paint (or even smaller amounts—some stores are now selling two-ounce containers of popular colors for this purpose), you can see exactly how a color will look. Just paint a fairly large expanse of wall (don't be shy—more is better), or prime and paint a sizable piece of plywood or posterboard in the color of your choice. (Two coats are better than one to give you an accurate color read; at the very least, make sure you let the initial coat dry completely before you assess the color.) Put the board in the room you intend to paint, and, moving it from wall to wall, observe it over a 24-hour period How does it look in the morning? Does it fade out in the noon sun? Does it turn gray and flat by lamplight? Will it work well as an accent but look overwhelming on all four walls?

When you're certain the color is right, purchase the full quantity of paint (with a little extra for future touch-ups) and break out the brushes and rollers.

green
to blue

yellow
to
green

blue
to
red

red to
yellow

The color wheel

The color wheel is a visual device that illustrates how colors relate to one another. Artists, printers, and cognitive scientists may put it to complex use, but in decorating terms, it's an excellent tool that allows us to understand at a glance how color families interact.

Primary colors—red, yellow, and blue—are at equidistant points on the wheel. All other colors can be made from these three.

Secondary colors are made by mixing the two primary colors on either side of them: orange, made of red and yellow; green, made of blue and yellow; and purple, made of blue and red.

Tertiary colors are made by combining a primary and a secondary color: Yellow and green make yellow-green; green and blue make teal; and so on.

The wheel also reflects variations of these colors in tone—darker tones with more gray in them are near the center, and lighter tones, containing more white, are closer to the outer edge.

Since white and black are not colors (technically, white is the presence of all color, black is the absence of all color), they do not appear on the color wheel. Yet when it comes to interior design, they are crucial: Black adds drama and definition; white, in its infinite guises, enhances other colors and is the foundation of many stylish palettes.

• Cool versus Warm. One of the wheel's most important functions is to illustrate cool and warm colors. Draw a line diagonally through the center of the circle, from red-violet to yellow-green. The colors on one side—greens, blues, and violets—are considered cool, reminding us of elements such as air and water. The colors on the other side—yellows, oranges, and reds—are considered warm, with their connection to earth, sun, and fire. As with everything pertaining to color, these distinctions are relative, affected by light and proximity to other hues. The categories aren't ironclad, but organizing colors this way is a valuable aid in building harmonious palettes.

• Color Relationships. Complementary colors—those directly opposite on the color wheel—intensify each other when they're paired. Red and green is a classic: A red Oriental rug in a room with pale green walls will give the space a vibrant, dynamic feel. These combinations are most successful when the colors are used in unequal proportions—an accent of yellow in a blue room, for example; using them in equal amounts sometimes makes them appear to vibrate.

Analogous colors are adjacent on the color wheel—yellow and green, for example, or blue and purple. These pairings tend to create harmonious, low-contrast, mellow schemes.

Monochromatic colors are different shades of a single color—layering blues from light to dark, for example. A room done in monochromatic shades is restful and calm, and can be very dramatic with the right accessories.

• Color Terms.

There are several more terms that are helpful: *Hue* is simply another word for "color."

Value refers to the relative lightness or darkness of a color, not to the color itself: Navy and burgundy have similar value, as do powder blue and baby pink. Colors of like value often work well together in a decorating scheme.

Intensity (also called "saturation") refers to the relative brightness or dullness of a color: The purer the color—the less it is diluted with another color—the more intense, or saturated, it is. Clear jewel tones such as teal, magenta, and ruby red are often described as saturated; they are effective both as accents and as dramatic overall room colors.

• Color by Color.

When we talk of red, blue, green, and so on, what we're really referring to is families of related colors that vary in intensity and value—green can be soft (sage, for example), bright (kelly), deep (hunter). On the following pages, we break down seven color families into several broad—though by no means exhaustive—variations: gray-blues, green-blues, red-blues, for example. Alongside each, we've given the names of Benjamin Moore® paint colors in that family, ranging in value from light to dark, to help you make the right choice in the paint store.

color by color

Pure or clean whites are formulated without any undertones to tint the finished coat. A favorite of designers looking for a backdrop to showcase art and furnishings, they include White; Super White; Decorators White.

Blue-green whites have a cool, crisp, breezy feel and blend well with equally cool colors from the blue and green side of the spectrum. These whites include Seafoam, 2123-60; Wedding Veil, 2125-70; Winter White, 2140-70; Mineral Ice, 2132-70; White Diamond, OC-61; Patriotic White, 2135-70.

Pink whites have a subtle rose or peachy blush that is flattering to faces and furnishings alike. They include Antique White; as well as Mirage White, 2116-70; Oyster, 2115-70; Moonlight White, OC-125; Pink Damask, OC-72; Opal, OC 73; Old Fashioned Peach, OC-79; Parchment OC-78.

Yellow whites are often described as warm, creamy, or buttery; these whites include Linen White, Navajo White, Cameo White; Mayonnaise, 2152-70; Lemon Ice, 2024-70; Antique Yellow, OC-103; Deserted Island, OC-99; Cream Froth, OC-97.

whites come in a staggering variety. A pure or "clean" white, which contains no deep pigments, is the whitest. Most others can be divided into two families: warm whites, with yellow, pink or brownish undertones; and cool whites, with minty green or blue-gray undertones.

Interior designed by Darryl Carter. **WALLS AND TRIM:** Moonlight White, OC-125.

grays are the chameleons of color—infinitely adaptable, at home in any color scheme. They always blend in and take on some of their neighbor's complementary shade: Gray next to red will look green, gray next to green will look red. This quality makes gray a true neutral, able to fade into the background and complement any decor.

Violet-grays reveal a dusky, amethyst tinge. Colors include Silver Dollar, 1460; Sea Life, 2118-40; Heaven, 2118-70; Misty Memories, 2118-60; Winter Gray, 2117-60; Dreamy Cloud, 2117-70; Full Moon, 2119-70.

Blue-grays have a cool, silvery, metallic quality. Colors in this family: Smoke, 2122-40; Little Falls, 1621; Manor Blue, 1627; New Hope Gray, 2130-50; Winter Lake, 2129-50; Misty Gray, 2124-60; Marilyn's Dress, 2125-60; Silver Half Dollar, 2121-40; Deep Silver, 2124-30.

True grays are the pale value of black, without colored undertones. Often used as an alternative to black, they make a crisp, lower-contrast pairing with white. They include Silver Lake, 1598; Boothbay Gray, HC-165; Seattle Gray, 2130-70; Mineral Ice, 2132-70; Sterling, 1591; Cobblestone Path, 1606; Rock Gray, 1615.

Mutable and complex, green-grays can have a warm, sagebrush glow or a cool, water-in-winter look. Colors include Raindance, 1572; Salisbury Green, HC-139; Homestead Green, AC-19; Cedar Mountains, 706; Antique Jade, 465; Quarry Rock, 1568; Carolina Gull, 2138-40; Green Tint, 2139-60.

Olive and putty grays can be a bridge color between warm and cooler shades, revealing hints of deep green and brown. In this family: Hampshire Gray, HC-101; Providence Olive, HC-98; Victorian Garden, 1531; Spanish Olive, 1509; November Rain, 2142-60; Antique Pewter, 1560; October Mist, 1495; Rockport Gray, HC-105; Castle Peak Gray, 1561.

The soft-gray family has yellow, taupe, and beige notes. Colors may include Waynesboro Taupe, 1544; Sag Harbor Gray, HC-95; Silver Fox, 2108-50; Cumulus Cloud, 1550; Vapor Trails, 1556; Richmond Gray, HC-96; Winter Orchard, 1555; Seattle Mist, 1535.

Brown-grays have a warm, rich quality. Colors include Smoked Oyster, 2109-40; Chelsea Gray, HC-168; Stardust, 2108-40; Fieldstone, 1558; Nimbus, 1465; Light Pewter, 1464; Equestrian Gray, 1553; Gray Huskie, 1473; Coastal Fog, 976; River Reflections, 1552.

Interior designed by Louis Aubert. **WALLS:** Victorian Garden, 1531.

Purple-browns have deep notes of cinnamon and burgundy—think of mocha and mauve. Colors include Townsend Harbor Brown, HC-64; Bison Brown, 2113-30; Incense Stick, 2115-20; Wisp of Mauve, 2098-60; Cinnamon Slate, 2113-40; Café Ole, 2098-40; Early Sunset, 2096-70; Wild Rice, 2097-70.

Reddish or orange-browns can range from rusty shades of brick and clay to light melon colors. These colors can be a good choice when you want a warm shade but are uncomfortable with bright red. In this family: Harvest Moon, 2167-30; Baked Terra Cotta, 1202; Georgian Brick, HC-50; Mexican Tile, 1194; Baker's Dozen, 1216; Corslbud Canyon, 076; Jumel Peachtone, HC-54; Antique Coral, 1198.

Leathery shades of tan range from frothy cappuccino to nut brown. Some shades have a coppery undertone. Colors include Saddle Tan, 1124; Marsh Brown, 2164-20; Tawny, 2161-20; Penny, 2163-30; Burlap, 2163-50; Adobe Beige, 1128; Plymouth Brown, HC-73; Havana Tan, 1121; October Sky, 2162-70; Lambskin, 1051.

Golden browns have strong yellow undertones and range from pale ivory to burnished bronze. Colors include Peanut Butter, 2159-20; Golden Dunes, 2157-10; Apple Crisp, 2159-30; Stuart Gold, HC-10; Hathaway Gold, 194; Bryant Gold, HC-7; Camel, 2165-10; Straw, 2154-50; Key West Ivory, 192; Old Gold, 167.

Beige-browns have a warm, creamy quality that makes them versatile neutrals. Colors in this family: Shelburne Buff, HC-28; Dunmore Cream, HC-29; Lighthouse Landing, 1044; Quincy Tan, HC-25; Powell Buff, HC-35; Waterbury Cream, HC-31; Philadelphia Cream, HC-30; Monroe Bisque, HC-26.

Yellow-browns sometimes have olive undertones, making them a natural bridge between yellows and greens. Colors include Brazen, 259; Corduroy, 2153-20; Livingston Gold, HC-16; Princeton Gold, HC-14; Norfolk Cream, 261; Woven Jacquard, 254; Henderson Buff, HC-15; Timothy Straw, 2149-40; Thyme, 2148-20; Sombrero, 249.

Taupes or gray-browns contain a lot of gray, making them easily adaptable partners for other colors, particularly grayed shades that share the same values. Colors in this family: Free Spirit, 245; Rustic Taupe, 999; Northampton Putty, HC-89; Hampshire Taupe, 990; Stone House, 1039; Brandy Cream, 1030; Litchfield Gray, HC-78; Greenbrier Beige, HC-79.

WALLS: Greenbrier Beige, HC-79; TRIM: White.

browns, full of nuance and depth, run from the rich, appetizing shades of chocolate and cinnamon to the calming tones of buff, taupe, and sand. Though their paler guises are often used to anchor neutral color schemes, the zestier shades of bronze, copper, and caramel are great on walls and trim as well. Used on a large scale, deep browns work best in rooms with abundant light, where the color reads true without shading to black.

green, the easiest color for the eye to see, is often thought of as calming and restful, though its more acidic, citrusy shades certainly pack a lively punch. Because it falls between blue and yellow on the color wheel, it makes a good bridge color that pairs well with both warm and cool palettes. Silvery sages, citrus greens, and dark, historic greens have seen a recent rise in popularity.

Olive and alligator greens have brownish undertones. Colors include Jalapeno Pepper, 2147-30; Avon Green, HC-126; Olive Moss, 2147-20; Mesquite, 501; Sweet Daphne, 529; Olive Branch, 2143-30; Sherwood Green, HC-118.

Yellow-greens can range from the famous avocado to acidic chartreuse. Colors in this category include Avocado, 2145-10; Limesickle, 2145-50; Split Pea, 2146-30; Brookside Moss, 2145-30; Soft Fern, 2144-40; Dried Parsley, 522; Chartreuse, 2024-10; Citron, 2024-30; Pale Sea Mist, 2147-50.

Lime and apple greens have a bright, contemporary feeling. Colors include Margarita, 2026-20; Tequila Lime, 2028-30; Dark Lime, 2027-10; Fresh Cut Grass, 2026-50; Summer Lime, 2026-60; Garland Green, 429; Neon Celery, 2031-60; Willow Springs Green, 418; Paradise Green, 2031-20.

These are the kelly greens, grass greens, and emeralds. In this family: Fresh Scent Green, 2033-30; Jade Green, 2037-20; Emerald Isle, 2039-20; Four Leaf Clover, 573; Leprechaun Green, 557; Lotus Flower, 571; Acadia Green, 2034-50; Marina Bay, 2036-50; Light Pistachio, 2034-60.

Warmer deep greens range from dark hunter green (a popular accent color) to light shades of eucalyptus. In low light, the deepest shades may read as black. Colors include Nile Green, 2035-30; Ming Jade, 2043-20; Forest Green, 2041-10; Deep Sea, 623; Key Largo Green, 620; Capri Seas, 2047-40; Italian Ice Green, 2035-70; Antigua Aqua, 610; Lido Green, 617.

Teal-greens include aquas and have an intense, almost luminous quality. Colors include Amelia Island Blue, 2044-40; Coastal Paradise, 655; Harbourside Teal, 654; Bahama Green, 2045-40; Blue Spa, 2052-40; Caribbean Cool, 661; Sea of Green, 657; Hannity Green, 646.

Blue-greens in this grouping are calmed by the addition of gray. Colors include Everglades, 641; Aberdeen Green, 631; Fresh Dew, 435; Scenic Drive, 697; Norway Spruce, 452; Garden Oasis, 699; Forest Valley Green, 634; Waterbury Green, HC-136; Covington Blue, HC-138.

Interior designed by Benjamin Noriega-Ortiz. **WALLS:** Garland Green, 429.

Blue- grays are a low-intensity alternative to brighter blues, delivering the cool color in a less vivid form. Colors include Niagara Falls, 1657; Alfresco, 1672; Hemlock, 719; Old Blue Jeans, 839; Whipple Blue, HC-152; Mediterranean Sky, 1662; Marlboro Blue, HC-153; Polar Ice, 1660; Glacier Blue, 1653.

This pale, watery blue family still has a hint of green; its shades feel gauzy and fresh. Colors include Delano Waters, 766; San Clemente Teal, 730; Sapphire Ice, 808; Splash, 2059-60; Crystal Springs, 764; Mystical Blue, 792; Little Boy Blue, 2061-60; Breath of Fresh Air, 806.

Teal-blues and turquoise-blues are almost equal parts green and blue and have a tropical feeling. Colors include Palm Coast Teal, 733; Blue Lagoon, 2054-40; Cool Aqua, 2056-40; Seaside Resort, 725; Seaside Blue, 2054-50; Turquoise Powder, 2057-50; Innocence, 2055-70; Clear Skies, 2054-70; Icy Moon Drops, 2056-70.

Royal blues build on a deep, primary blue base. Lighter shades are the classic powder blue and baby blue. In this family: Ol' Blue Eyes, 2064-30; Dark Royal Blue, 2065-20; Midnight Navy, 2067-10; Toronto Blue, 2060-40; Light Blue, 2066-70; Blue Marguerite, 2063-50; Athens Blue, 797; Bluebelle, 2064-60.

Often described as periwinkle or lavender blue, shades in this family are warmed by notes of red and violet. Colors include Brazilian Blue, 817; Blue Pearl, 1433; Spring Flowers, 1430; Lavender Blue, 1438; Violet Dusk, 1409; Misty Blue, 820; Aqua Marina, 816; Sweet Bluette, 813.

Violet, lilac, lavender—these lighter, cooler violets are influenced more by blue than by red. Violet is another effective "bridge" color, working well with both cool and warm palettes. Colors include Seduction, 1399; Persian Violet, 1419; English Hyacinth, 1417; French Lilac, 1403; Lavender Mist, 2070-60; Spring Lilac, 1388; Lily Lavender, 2071-60; Nosegay, 1401.

Purples and plums are very powerful, warm colors, sometimes bordering on pink in their lighter notes. Colors include Twilight Magenta, 2074-30; Pink Raspberry, 2075-40; Summer Plum, 2074-20; Plum Perfect, 1371; Purple Easter Egg, 2073-50; Passion Pink, 2075-60; Luscious, 1369.

Interior designed by Benjamin Noriega-Ortiz. **WALLS:** Misty Blue, 820.

blue is often cited as America's favorite color. Quintessentially cool—the color of ice, snow, and water—blues also offer warmer variations as they move toward the lavender end of the spectrum. Pair blue with greens and minty whites for an icy, refreshing palette; spike it with dashes of a complementary red or yellow to warm or enliven its coolness.

red always makes a statement. In its lighter, brighter incarnations, it is energetic, powerful, stimulating. In its darker tones, it feels rich, warm, and luxurious. Saturated jewel tones of hot pink and magenta add sophisticated style and sparkle to a decor, while coral and salmon tones evoke tropical climates. Deep reds are a good choice in rooms used by night, such as formal dining rooms.

Violet-reds are often described as magenta, orchid, and fuchsia. Lighter tones include airy baby pinks and roses, while darker tones have an exotic, feminine punch. In this family: Gypsy Pink, 2077-20; Peony, 2079-30; Cranberry Ice, 1362; Raspberry Mousse, 2076-40; Paradise Pink, 2078-40; I Love You Pink, 2077-70; Peppermint, 1359.

Burgundy and cranberry shades often feel at home in historic or traditional interiors. Colors include Cranberry Cocktail, 2083-20; Plum Raisin, 2082-20; Gypsy Love, 2085-30; Rosewood, 2082-40; Rose Rococo, 1275; Powder Blush, 1388; Tara, 1270.

Bright bubblegum pinks have many gradations, from the little-girl pink of ballet slippers to powerful pink popsicle. Cooler than strong reds, these pinks still read as warm. In this family are Bubble Bath, 1326; True Pink, 2003-40; Springtime Bloom, 2079-40; Pink Lace, 2081-60; Cat's Meow, 1332; Pink Eraser, 2005-50; Marshmallow Bunny, 2001-70.

Bright reds are very strong colors best used in small doses or as an accent. Colors include Red, 2000-10; Candy Cane Red, 2079-10; Raspberry Truffle, 2080-10; Mediterranean Spice, 1337; Cherry Wine, 2080-30; Confederate Red, 2080-20; Cactus Flower, 1335.

Salmon pinks and coral reds contain a lot of orange, giving them a peachy complexion. Colors include Tucson Coral, 005; Passion Fruit, 2171-40; Perky Peach, 2012-50; Bermuda Pink, 016; Coral Reef, 012; Sunlit Coral, 2170-60; Salmon Peach, 2013-50; Dusk Pink, 2013-40.

Rust reds and ochers have even deeper brown and orange tones. In this family: Rosy Peach, 2089-20; Santa Fe Pottery, 1287; Peach Cobbler, 2169-40; Orange Creamsickle, 059; Fruited Plains, 029; Navajo Red, 2171-10; Spanish Red, 1301; Adobe Orange, 2171-30; Nautilus Shell, 064.

Interior designed by Birch Coffey. **WALLS AND TRIM:** Navajo Red, 2171-10.

Colors in the red-orange category include intense shades of mango and cantaloupe. Among these are Orange Froth, 151; Fruity Cocktail, 147; Tangelo, 2017-30; Tangy Orange, 2014-30; Orange Burst, 2015-20; Festive Orange, 2014-10; Orange Juice, 2017-10; Peach Sorbet, 2015-40.

Pale oranges are often described in fruity terms, such as peach and apricot. These colors impart a healthy glow to the skin, making them popular in baths and bedrooms. They include Marmalade, 2016-40; Peach Crisp, 159; Tangerine Zing, 132; Orange Sherbet, 122; Delicate Peach, 120; Juno Peach, 087; Melon Popsicle, 2016-50; Cancun Sand, 2016-70; Georgia On My Mind, 134.

As cheery as an egg fried sunny-side up, warm orange-yellows range from marigold to sunflower. Colors in this family: Lemon Shine, 2020-20; Nacho Cheese, 2018-40; Sunflower, 2019-30; Mandarin Orange, 2018-20; Aura, 169; American Cheese, 2019-40.

Golden yellows have warm, brownish tones like those in honey and amber. Colors in this family: Showtime, 293; Glen Ridge Gold, 301; Goldfield, 292; Golden Lab, 178; Precious Ivory, 185; Hawthorne Yellow, HC-4; Morning Light, 183; Halifax Cream, 344; Candlelit Dinner, 295.

Bright, pure yellows are very powerful, luminous colors that draw attention to themselves. Colors include Yellow, 2022-10; Yellow Rain Coat, 2020-40; Lemon, 2021-20; Sun Porch, 2023-30; Sunburst, 2023-40; Delightful Yellow, 335.

Buttery yellows are less powerful than pure yellows but have a warm, glowing quality. Colors in this family: Wildflowers, 325; Good Morning Sunshine, 326; Amarillo, 320; Pale Moon, 289; Butter, 2023-60; Yellow Lotus, 2021-50.

Yellow-greens range from intense, citrus-flavored accents to muted, almost neutral mustards. Colors include Bright Gold, 371; Citrus Burst, 364; Mustard Field, 377; Calla Lily, 283; Treasure Trove, 285; Yellow Roses, 353; St Elmo's Fire, 362; Mulholland Yellow, 369; Citronee, 281; Falling Star, 351.

WALLS: St. Elmo's Fire, 362; TRIM: White.

yellow—warm, cheerful, uplifting—may feel too intense in large quantities, so consider using it several shades paler than you think you want. Paired with green, yellow softens; paired with blue or violet, it brightens. Pale yellows give the illusion of daylight in light-deprived spaces. Intense orange can be a difficult color to live with; consider softer shades of apricot, peach, and mango.

JUST AS COLORS ON A COLOR STRIP

come alive on a wall, color palettes come alive in a home. Reading about tints, tones, and intensities is helpful in theory, but the true test is how colors react in a real-life setting.

On the following pages are profiles of homes intended to intrigue, inform, and inspire. Each offers a look at a unique color environment, influenced by light and surroundings, shaped by individual style. Many have been fashioned by leading American designers. They range from a tiny New York

color inspirations

City apartment to a spacious 9,000-square-foot mansion on Washington, D.C.'s Embassy Row; from a 200-year-old farmhouse to a clean-lined seaside contemporary. The use of color is as varied as the architecture. There are mellow palettes based entirely on a single shade of warm white; saturated jewel tones of magenta and chartreuse; calming interiors of soft, gray-green neutrals.

The exact colors used are identified in photo captions, but it's important to remember that the rich chocolate brown you admire in a light-filled photo may look entirely different in your bedroom or study. As always, the acid test is trying a sample out on your walls. Whether a particular color will look as good in your home as it does on the page depends on comparable exposure and light, equivalent architectural style, and similar furnishings and flooring.

Light, bright, and white

ANYONE LOOKING AT THE LIGHT-FILLED,

luxurious retreat that designer Vicente Wolf created out of a Long Island carriage house would scarcely believe the home's dark, cramped beginnings. Yet when the owners first approached him, the turn-of-the-century structure could best be described as oppressive. "The mission here was to open and lighten everything," Wolf says.

Using his signature white palette and sensuous layering of texture, he set about transforming the space. Work began in the entrance hall, where the front door was pushed out and the enclosure enlarged to the edge of the original stoop. Glass panes usher in the views and light from the extensive gardens. Limestone floors create a pale neutral base, and Wolf chose a single tint of clean, unshaded white to cover the walls, trim, and ceiling.

The same white is carried into the living and dining rooms, situated on either side of the foyer, where it is softened by rich fabrics in tones of camel and leather, with a romantic sweep of floor-to-ceiling curtains in taupe wool. Hand-woven, antique Burmese fabrics spice up the calm, restful palette, as do splashes of yellow on pillows and dining room chairs. On the second floor, two small bedrooms are now a floor-through master suite, with the bed at one end and a sitting area at the other. Wolf chose a cool, blue-cast white, wrapping the color around walls and trim, to emphasize the room's spacious, airy quality.

The large entry foyer now basks in sunlight, after the front walls were extended and replaced with glass. The clean white walls and ceiling take on a cooling, greenish cast in summer, when light filters through the surrounding foliage. The console is an antique Chinese altar table, carved to resemble bamboo.
WALLS AND TRIM: Super White.

Although the palette is subdued, the living room (left and opposite above) is such a rich panoply of textures that the eye is constantly engaged. The pure white, used throughout the first floor, works well on its own; paired with other shades of white—particularly creamy or beige tones—it makes its partners look muddy. The small painting on the end table is a nineteenth-century Indian piece done on glass. The coffee table is a Chinese antique.

WALLS AND TRIM: Super White.

The living room color scheme is repeated in the dining room (opposite below), to integrate and enlarge both spaces. Use of the same fabrics, from the taupe curtains to the yellow accents, creates a soothing visual symmetry. The chairs are an artfully arranged jumble, mixing Indian and Chinese antiques with classic upholstered shapes.

WALLS AND TRIM: SUPER White.

The secret to the sensual appeal of this home is the sumptuous use of rich texture and layered neutral shades, both of which soften the starkness of pure white. Striking Asian antiques throughout, collected by the designer during frequent buying trips abroad, leap out dramatically against the monochromatic white backdrop. "Clean whites don't tint their surroundings," Wolf says. "But they pick up the tonality of the light, and that can be very dynamic."

"I LIKE SOME ROOMS TO HAVE A
SENSE OF ROMANCE." —VICENTE WOLF

Wolf's signature whites are pure, or "clean," with no deep pigments to create pink or blue undertones. These bright whites work well in rooms with an abundance of natural light, where they won't turn dim or flat. Bright whites make neutral beiges and grays appear darker by contrast, and cool colors look fresh and crisp. Be wary of pairing them with beige-tinted antique whites, which can look dirty by comparison. Because all white palettes lead the eye to focus on texture and line, consider building your room around touchable fabrics and sculptural furnishings.

French doors in the master suite (opposite), with its large windows on three sides, open onto a small balcony. The cool, blue-toned white keeps the room feeling fresh in the day-long flood of sun. The bed is of Wolf's own design; the curtains are a tarnished-silver silk. **WALLS AND TRIM:** Patriotic White, 2135-70.

The bedroom sitting area (above) is a sensuous retreat of curvaceous surfaces and soft lines. Wolf designed the rug; the sculpture is an antique hand of Buddha from Thailand. **WALLS AND TRIM:** Patriotic White, 2135-70.

Focus on furnishings

The coffered walls of the main stairwell (opposite) are painted a high-gloss black, and stair treads are picked out in black deck paint. The high-contrast effect infuses the otherwise ordinary space with drama and monumentality. The mullions of glass-paned doors in a back hallway (above) are outlined in black, adding a strong, graphic element to a simple corridor.

WALLS: Decorators White;
TRIM: Black.

WHEN DESIGN ENTREPRENEUR MICHAEL Bruno bought his four-bedroom 1915 farmhouse in the Hamptons, on New York's Long Island, he had two goals. One was simply to enjoy the surroundings—the traditional center hall architecture, the six acres of rolling hills, the extensive garden and stone terraces. The other was to make it a testing ground for his new venture, an online gallery of fine antiques and furnishings from dealers in the United States and Europe.

The house, he had decided, was to be outfitted entirely through cyberspace, using his own Web site, 1stdibs.com, to locate and purchase everything from chests to chairs. He was in New York; much of the furniture would be shipped from Paris. "My house was the test run to see if the site worked," he says. That process meant the rooms had to be painted and finished before the arrival of the furnishings, which would spend weeks in transit. Bruno's approach was to prepare the 3,000-square-foot house like a stage set, in anticipation of props and cast of characters to come. The wood floors throughout were stained a dark mahogany, to ground the rooms and keep furniture from visually "floating." The stairwell was painted a deep glossy black to throw into relief its handsome architectural lines. Walls were done in a uniform clean white to create an unobtrusive, museumlike backdrop for showcasing furniture. The only departure was the dining room, where the walls were painted a soft dove gray to complement the silvery mirrors and the marble-topped sideboard that would eventually reside there.

The result is a stylish environment, flexible enough to accommodate the most eclectic of tastes. Since the clean white used in many

With its pitched roof and drafts-manlike desk, the upstairs library (left) is a luxurious play on a Parisian garret. The room is painted a warm, coffee-tinted cream, but next to the dark floor and black-and-white accents it reads as white. The natural tones of wicker, wood, and bamboo keep the room from feeling stark. **WALLS AND TRIM:** Seapearl, OC-19.

The spacious living room (opposite) has two sets of French doors that lead onto a stone terrace, with views of the garden beyond. Except for the occasional animal print, pattern is kept to a minimum; instead, the symmetrical placement of furniture and the sculptural lines of the pieces create their own visual rhythm. The dark floors are intentionally left bare to send the gaze upward. **WALLS AND TRIM:** Decorators White.

rooms is formulated with no deep pigment, it has no colored undertones to influence its surroundings, making it infinitely adaptable. In the living room, now filled with 1940s French furnishings, the black-and-white scheme has a sophisticated, formal, salonlike flavor. In the kitchen, warmed by wood countertops and domestic clutter, the same dark-floor, white-wall combination takes on a cozy, country feel.

"My last house had lots of color," Bruno says. "Here, I wanted a quiet, museumlike space, one that would let the furnishings take the starring role."

"THEY CALL IT DECORATORS WHITE BECAUSE IT'S
THE PERFECT BACKGROUND COLOR." —MICHAEL BRUNO

The kitchen (opposite), with its preference for furniture over fitted cabinetry, has an eclectic, mix-and-match appeal. The massive table in the center was bought online from a Paris flea market. A bistro mirror above the stove helps pull the view of the garden indoors. The breakfast room (above) is outfitted with nineteenth-century steel park chairs. Against the white beadboard walls, the effect is as fresh as a Paris café in spring.

WALLS AND TRIM: Decorators White.

The soft gray of the dining room walls (right) is less of a contrast to the dark floor than the stark white used elsewhere. The walls seem to fade away, enlarging the space and leaving the eye to focus on the decorative elements. The eighteenth-century dining table is of Cuban mahogany, bought online from Brussels; the octagonal mirror above the sideboard came from a home in Normandy.

WALLS: Horizon OC-53;
TRIM: Decorators White.

A whiter shade of pale

AT 9,000 SQUARE FEET, THIS HISTORIC town house on Washington D.C.'s Embassy Row was an intimidating space to tackle. Its former life as the Chancery of Oman had left it with dropped acoustic ceilings, acres of hospital-gray carpet, and a nuke-proof panic room with a commercial-size document shredder. Designer Darryl Carter can be excused for feeling some trepidation.

Yet as a potential residence, the building had many appealing characteristics. The front rooms have extraordinary views of the neighborhood's handsome architecture; in the back are vistas of leafy parkland, as verdant as it gets in the city center.

For Carter, who had been searching for a flat-front structure with high, square rooms devoid of Victorian frippery, the bones of this building fit the bill. "I looked at the place grudgingly, under duress, and felt it was too cavernous," he recalls. "But the site, the light, the limestone façade, won me over. Then the challenge was to make it more intimate."

The first step was to divide the four-story house into private and public quarters. The ground level became a studio and office, which house Carter's design and furniture businesses. The upper floors were converted into living areas, with the grand foyer and library on the first floor; the kitchen, breakfast room, dining room, and living room on the second; a self-contained gym, media room, and master bedroom suite on the third; and three guest bedrooms and baths on the fourth.

The next step was to pull all those levels together. A lawyer by training, Carter brought some of the discipline and logic of his former profession to his design aesthetic. To that end, he chose a single

In a corner of the living room (opposite), mellow white walls and trim, free of pink or yellow undertones, are grounded by the espresso-toned wood floors and dark mantel. A Louis XIV chair upholstered in burlap supplies surprising contrast. The monumental foyer (above) is dominated by art, including two oversize framed pieces by Catherine Lauerman. The space's simple white palette forms a discreet envelope, drawing the eye upward from the creamy limestone floors to the 12-foot-high ceilings.
WALLS AND TRIM: Moonlight White, OC-125; **DOORS IN FOYER:** Black, 2132-10.

French doors in the breakfast room (opposite) let in a flood of morning light. Walls are painted a delicate, washed-out blue ("I love how the color changes with the light," says Carter), which creates a backdrop for his collection of creamy white ironstone. The wood tones of the antique pine table seem to glow in the cool surroundings.
WALLS: Woodlawn Blue, HC-147;
TRIM: Moonlight White, OC-125.

The backs of the custom-milled kitchen cabinets (right), painted in the same blue as the breakfast room, set off a collection of blue-and-white flow-ware. Cabinet doors are done in decorative mesh for added texture and patina. In keeping with his pared-down taste, Carter replaced an ornate mantel with a plain wooden one pulled from a Virginia farmhouse and stained black.
WALLS AND TRIM: Moonlight White, OC-125; **CABINET INTERIORS:** Woodlawn Blue, HC-147.

shade of warm white for the entire house (diverging only once, in the pale blue breakfast/sun room). The largely monochromatic color scheme unites the spaces and creates a clean, quiet background for his eclectic art collection.

For contrast and drama, the designer used dark wood furnishings (many from the Darryl Carter Home Collection) interspersed with antiques; dark wood floors stained a coffee color throughout; and unexpected textures such as the reverse side of rugs, which reveals their muted patterns, and sheer linen curtains banded in rich velvet.

"I like spaces that transition seamlessly," Carter says. His new home does just that—to perfection.

The bathroom (above) displays the designer's passion for symmetry: The tub simply cried out for a mate. A converted farm table was fitted with sinks, and a pair of old government-issue cabinets was stripped, stained, and filled with white linens. The dark lines of the furnishings add depth and shadow to the all-white room.

WALLS: Moonlight White, OC-125; **TRIM:** Simply White, OC-117.

The master bedroom (opposite) boasts rich layers of texture: rough sisal rug, cashmere-like curtains, sheared chenille and linen bedding. The classical-inspired four-poster bed is from the Darryl Carter Home Collection. Between bed and window is a thrashing board studded with agate. As in the rest of the house, the palette puts the focus on shapes and surfaces.

WALLS AND TRIM: Moonlight White, OC-125.

"NEUTRAL PALETTES CAN BE FAR MORE COMPLEX THAN PEOPLE IMAGINE."
—DARRYL CARTER

"THIS IS MY VERSION OF A FISHERMAN'S SHACK." —STEVEN GAMBREL

The fireplace in the great room (left) is new, but matte black paint on the brick gave it instant age. Ceilings soar to 15 feet, adding vertical dimension to the small space; the walls are all done in wide beadboard. The stuffed fish was hooked right off a friend's wall; the ladder to the left of it leads to a sleeping loft.
WALLS: Gray Owl, 2137-60;
TRIM: Sea Haze, 2137-50; Carolina Gull, 2138-40.

The beadboard walls of the kitchen (opposite) are painted a dusty French blue to provide a pool of shade for summertime meals. Entering the room from the light-filled living area beyond provokes a steep drop in visual temperature; the doors (unseen) are painted a deep navy to help the transition.
WALLS: Summer Blue, 2067-50;
TRIM: White; **DOOR**: Deep Royal, 2061-10.

Perfection by the bay

●●●●●●●●●●

THIS DOLLHOUSE OF A COTTAGE SITS

right on a cove, only 30 feet up from the high-tide mark. Sailboats are moored outside the windows, ducks paddle in the water, and kayaks can be pulled ashore to the back door.

That location made the structure worth saving, though it was little more than a nondescript fifties shack when designers Chris Connor and Steven Gambrel took it in hand. Using a nineteenth-century prototype of a typical fisherman's house, they rebuilt it from the ground up, replacing windows and reproportioning the interior. Only 600 square feet, the space now functions beautifully as a weekend cottage. The shipshape layout consists of a living room with fireplace, bedroom with a view, small kitchen, bath, and upstairs sleeping alcove.

Given the surroundings, the colors and objects can't help being influenced by the water of the cove lapping at the rocks. In fact, from the captain's chairs to the tide charts to the big-mouthed bass mounted above the mantel, the decor is spiked with maritime ephemera. The colors, however, are less predictable. While the conventional choice would have been a nautical blue-and-white color scheme, Gambrel and Connor clothed the rooms in a brown-based owl-wing gray. Because light bouncing off water has a strong blue cast, which tinges any white around it, the designers made a conscious decision not to use pure

The colors in the living room progress from darkest on trim to lightest on walls: Window casements are a dark putty, the frames slightly lighter, and so on until you arrive at the soft gray-brown stone shade on the walls. A rope chart, shells, and other nautical flotsam decorate the cottage in a lighthearted tribute to the seaside setting.
WALLS: Gray Owl, 2137-60;
TRIM: Sea Haze, 2137-50;
Carolina Gull, 2138-40.

Water reflects about 50 percent more light than land does and absorbs much of the red in sunlight as well. Thus the light that pours in the windows of any seaside house will have a strong blue tint, turning all whites to blue-gray and pushing greens to the cool side of the spectrum. Painting the walls a warm, sandy color balances the flood of blue while mimicking the pairing of sand, sea, and sky.

whites. The putty tones they chose for most of the rooms read much lighter in the wash of reflected sunlight than on a color chip, and their warmer undertones counteract the push toward the cooler end of the spectrum. The earthy colors also feel like an extension of the natural materials used throughout the cottage: All the walls are wood beadboard rather than drywall, and the shells and sea grass, twig furniture, and driftwood look as though they could have been the early-morning finds of a lucky beachcomber.

The wallpaper in the stairwell was ordered from a London firm that has been producing the stylized stone pattern for the past 150 years. All trim, crown moldings, and cabinetry throughout the house are painted one of two popular, ready-mixed whites, as a way of integrating the rambling spaces.

TRIM: Linen White; Antique White.

Inspired by tradition

WHEN JOCK AND ALEXANDRA SPIVY
decided their gracious Italianate villa needed a thorough overhaul, they knew that maintaining the structure's historic integrity would be of prime importance. They also knew they had no intention of living in a museum. Instead, they wanted a warm and inviting setting for weekends, as well as an appropriate backdrop for their extensive collection of nineteenth-century American furnishings and art. The couple relied on their own broad knowledge of the decorative arts (Alexandra is an art historian), as well as the expertise of a nationally known historic restoration firm, to come up with a plan that met both needs.

Situated on the edge of a historic village in New York's Hudson Valley, the house was built in 1854 by a wealthy manufacturer. It was extensively remodeled in 1925, at which time ceilings were lowered, bedrooms subdivided, and wiring and plumbing replaced. The Spivys did two years of research before undertaking their own renovation project, the goal of which was to upgrade all mechanical systems, undo the remodeling indignities, and restore the house to its original, high-ceilinged, Victorian loveliness.

The completed home provides a primer on how to be inspired, rather than intimidated, by historic colors. The yellow-toned cream in the living room, for example, was chosen because many 1850s houses featured light colors and the oil-based paint tended to yellow with age. (It was only after the Civil War that the heavy, dark colors we associate with Victorian interiors became fashionable.) The dining room may most closely resemble its original incarnation: A shade similar to the rich

By picking up the marble tones of the mantelpiece, the greenish-gray walls in the library provide a calm backdrop for a collection of nineteenth-century white marble busts. **WALLS:** November Rain, 2142-60; **DOORS, TRIM, AND CABINETRY:** Linen White, 70;. **CROWN MOLDINGS AND CORNICES:** Antique White, 75.

rose on the walls was unearthed during renovations and reproduced at the paint store. On the other hand, the antique reproduction wallpaper in the stairwell was paired with simple white trim, and the mid-tone gray in the library was chosen more for its soothing qualities than for its period precision. The main objective, the owners emphasize, was to avoid glaring anachronisms, rather than be slaves to a limited palette.

Throughout the home, the space is anchored and unified by dark wood floors of quarter-sawn oak, and trim colors are held to two creamy whites; both provide continuous visual threads. The overall feeling is one of timeless serenity and approachable elegance, in keeping with the house's grand old bones.

During renovation of the dining room, the Spivys dug through layers of wall covering. The earliest shade they struck was a deep rose. While they might not have been brave enough to call for such a color on their own, the historical evidence was persuasive (though not absolute, as time can substantially alter paint colors), and the paint was ordered. As it turns out, the warm, rosy hues look wonderful at night. "This is a great dinner-party room," says Jock Spivy. "Everyone looks so healthy." The rich shade also makes a fabulous backdrop for the couple's collection of rare sandpaper paintings of the Hudson Valley, with their stark shades of black, white, and gray.

WALLS: Pink Peach, 2009-40;
TRIM: Linen White; Antique White.

"ANYONE WHO HAS A PERIOD HOUSE SHOULD DO SOME HOMEWORK—RESEARCH AND PLANNING MAKE ALL THE DIFFERENCE."

—JOCK SPIVY

The living room (left) is filled with dappled light filtered through the house's deep wraparound porch. The pale, creamy white on the walls reinforces the calm and luminous quality of the room—a strong contrast to the dark, intricate outlines of the Gothic-style chairs and bookcase, once owned by Daniel Webster.
WALLS: Philadelphia Cream, HC-30; **TRIM:** Linen White; Antique White.

The kitchen (opposite) is painted a slightly warmer, richer yellow to make the most of the room's abundant natural light.
WALLS: Morning Sunshine, 2018-50; **TRIM:** Linen White; Antique White.

Restoring a period house is a labor of love, not an obligation bound by rules. Begin by doing preliminary research: Peek under wallpaper, sand down a patch of wall, contact your local historical society, consult your paint dealer about available colors, or hire an expert if you have the time and budget. But don't feel imprisoned by the information you uncover. Contemporary colors can allude, rather than adhere, to historic palettes.

Complex colors in a simple setting

● ● ● ● ● ● ● ● ● ● ●

Daylight tends to flatter the cooler aspects of the complex palette in the entry (above); the simple act of switching on a lamp can shift the entire wall color to a warmer shade.
ENTRY WALLS: Sandy White 2148-50; **TRIM:** Antique White.

Constantly shifting between blue, green, and brownish undertones depending on angle and light, the smoky color of the large living room (opposite) is hard to define. The stone-colored trim warms the space just a notch and ties it to the other ground-floor living areas.
WALLS: Cornstalk, 542;
TRIM: Calm, 2111-70.

COLOR MAY BE THE MOST IMPORTANT furnishing in this East Coast Georgian-style house, built in 1780. The intriguing blue-green of the living room, the rich biscuit color of the central hall, the layered stone and clay colors on trim—each room is a unique color environment, suffused with ambiguous, complex shades that call you back for a second look.

The house was redone during the Greek Revival period of the 1800s, and needed a thorough updating by the time it passed into the current owner's hands. His fondness for spare, Scandinavian interiors influenced many of the choices, from the stripped wood floors to the unadorned windows. That uncluttered aesthetic pays tribute to the home's spartan Colonial past while feeling thoroughly modern—a trick accomplished by the informal mix of antique and contemporary furnishings and the use of a highly complex color palette.

Compared with simple pastels or primaries, complex colors contain a greater number of complementary pigments and react more variably to light. Here, the blue-green of the living room glows almost lavender in the morning, whispers blue at midday, and settles into gray green at night. The complex greens, deep golds, and earth tones were created through trial and error: Each room was painted several times, and the shade was adjusted until it matched the desired mood. The trim colors in the master bedroom, for example, came from gradually adding splashes of brown to the soft sage green on the walls. The resulting shades are dense, even cerebral, shifting from one end of the spectrum to the other according to the time of day and season.

Bare floors, spare furnishings, and complex colors are the core of this look. Nonwhite neutrals on trim and woodwork tie the spaces together; shifting, evocative shades on walls keep things visually interesting. Since the depth and mutable nature of the colors are revealed by the play of light, these complex shades work best in rooms with lots of natural daylight, where they can react to the movement of the sun and the seasons of the year. (Colors look as different in the leafy green light of summer and the flat, gray light of winter as they do in morning and night light.)

The master bedroom (left) is built around a sage-green palette, with walls, mantel, and trim all done in tonal variations: gray-green on the walls, then browner, earthier shades on the trim and mantelpiece. The monochromatic scheme is an interesting play on the spare Colonial style. In one corner (opposite) a door leads into a small all-white study. The muted greens of the bedroom intensify in proximity to the white walls beyond, and the white picks up a reflected, greenish cast.

WALLS: Saybrook Sage, HC-114;
TRIM: Louisburg Green, HC-113;
Kennebunkport Green, HC-123.

The parchment-like, baked-biscuit color of the front hall (opposite) acts as the anchor for the whole house, the one shade all the others relate to. It was the first color the owner picked, inspired by a similar shade in a historic house in Virginia.
WALLS: Sandy White, 2148-50; **TRIM:** Antique White.

The dining room (right) does double duty as a second sitting room. Warm yellow-orange walls soak up the strong sunshine by day and reflect it back at night. The cheery color also acts as a welcome, beckoning guests from the hallway.
WALLS: Stuart Gold, HC-10; **TRIM:** Calm, 2111-70.

Going with the flow

THERE'S A TIMELESS, UNHURRIED QUALITY
to the spacious rooms of this turn-of-the-century home, but when the new owners called Boston-based designers Cheryl and Jeffrey Katz, things weren't so calm: The family of four had one month to vacate their old home and get the new one ready for occupancy.

In a sense, the rush was serendipitous. The time constraints forced the designers to develop an all-encompassing, top-to-bottom color palette for the house (and to hire three paint crews to put it in place on deadline). The result is an unusually integrated, composed color scheme, with the serene sage-greens, browns, and grays used in the house's public areas flowing into one another as naturally as water.

The monumental scale of the first floor influenced the particular color choices. The large living room, dining room, and den all open onto a soaring center hall, and the wide arches and open doorways mean that each room is visible from the others. The open sight lines lend additional importance to a coherent color environment, where hues of similar value rub shoulders harmoniously. The designers cite the work of forties fashion icon Charles James as an inspiration: "His gowns were so beautiful because he used many colors of similar value—the colors could mix because they were all bound with gray," says Jeffrey Katz. "We try to do the same in our own work."

In fact, the silvery grays, which give the living room a sophisticated, urbane, 1930s feel, morph right into the putty and sage (both tempered with gray) used in the hall and den, keeping the eye from halting at any conspicuous color break.

The grand sweep of the formal front hall (opposite) and the traditional layout of the living areas (above) are saved from forbidding elegance by the choice of paint colors. Complex gray- and green-based neutrals feel more contemporary than the setting, and bridge the gap between the period architecture and the informal mix of modern furnishings.
HALL: Gray Mirage, 2142-50;
LIVING ROOM: Camouflage, 2143-40; **TRIM**: White Dove, OC-17.

"WHEN ALL ROOMS ARE OPEN TO EACH OTHER, THE COLORS HAVE TO BE LINKED AS WELL." —JEFFREY KATZ

The living room (opposite) is a sophisticated mix of tone-on-tone silver and pewter-grays. The den (right) uses two warm red leather chairs to pull the eye in. The powder room (below) is clad in sumptuous veined marble, with a rich taupe on the upper half of the wall that picks up the gold-leaf tones in the mirror frame. To further enhance the enveloping quality of these rooms, all the ceilings are painted the same color as the walls, cut with two or three parts white to lighten and heighten the space overhead. Trim is painted a uniform warm, dusty white throughout the house.
LIVING ROOM: Camouflage, 2143-40; **DEN:** Lenox Tan, HC-44; **POWDER ROOM:** Whitall Brown, HC 69; **TRIM:** White Dove, OC-17.

Upstairs, where the bedrooms are private and can be closed off from view, the designers felt free to use playful, stand-alone shades. The doors provide a clear visual break, so each room can work as a unique color environment. As a result, the children's rooms and play area, where strong colors are let off the leash, are light, bright, and full of fun. "Color is a way to add instant design and architecture," says Jeffrey Katz. "You can make kids' rooms as simple or as whimsical as you want—there isn't the same imperative to relate the rooms to the rest of the house."

The designers had free rein to invent colorful, kid-friendly spaces upstairs. The girl's room (opposite) uses two bright panels of apple green to create visual alcoves for the twin beds.
WALLS: Celadon Green, 2028-60; Pear Green, 2028-40; **TRIM:** White Dove, OC-17.

The spacious children's play area (right) was created under the third-floor eaves. Chalkboard paint covers one entire wall to accommodate spontaneous artistic urges.
WALLS: Sapphireberry, 2063-60; Celadon Green, 2028-60; **TRIM:** White Dove, OC-17; Chalkboard paint.

The boy's room (below) is a cheerful combination of lavender and blue, the lavender acting to warm the large expanse of cooler color.
WALLS: Summer Blue, 2067-50; Blue Orchid, 2069-50; **TRIM:** White Dove, OC-17.

"CHILDREN'S ROOMS CALL OUT FOR STRONGER, MORE PLAYFUL HUES."

—JEFFREY KATZ

Cool southern style

In the living room/dining room (above), the walls and trim are painted all one color to avoid an overdose of detail. The sideboard is an 1840s plantation piece, topped with white Cararra marble.
WALLS AND TRIM:
Ice Formations, 973.

The floor of the sunroom (opposite) is painted a slate gray pulled from the slate landing outside; the spring green of the bookcases was inspired by the clipped boxwood hedge in the yard. A nineteenth-century Balinese monkey stands guard.
WALLS: French White, 1093;
BOOKCASE: Folk Art, 528.

NEW ORLEANS' PRESTIGIOUS TREE-LINED

"park" streets, the turn-of-the-century equivalent of a gated community, haven't changed much over the last century: tall oaks, minimal traffic, period architecture. When designer, colorist, and New Orleans native Louis Aubert bought a 1917 Arts and Crafts bungalow on one of those streets ten years ago, he wanted to respect that timeless, unhurried quality. He conceived of the classic, one-level house as an Anglo-colonial outpost in the tropics, bathed in cooling colors to deflect the powerful heat, filled with art and exotic artifacts, and related to the outdoors through the deep filter of porches and overhangs.

The soft shades Aubert chose for the interior blend well with the hazy southern light and are designed to move seamlessly from room to room. The cool pewter color in the living and dining room spills over into the hall, where it's used as a base for a subtle, tone-on-tone striped effect; the creamy almond tone of the kitchen reappears in the front study, where it's paired with the palest of pale-green ceilings, casting a cool shadow over a room that gets afternoon light.

A new addition to the back of the house blends into the home's original profile. Jutting into the garden, the sunroom/study boasts a wall of bookshelves in a bright spring green. The colors and view give the sense of being outdoors, and the almond shade of the surrounding walls links the room to the older portion of the home.

"There's a lot of cross-pollination between the rooms, which is wise in a small house," Aubert says. "When you repeat the same shades, the space enlarges around you."

"A GREEN CEILING IS LIKE THE UNDERSIDE OF A LEAF, VERY COOLING." —LOUIS AUBERT

A charming jumble of objects and styles enlivens the guest bedroom/library (opposite). The Indonesian daybed is upholstered in an old chenille bedspread, reversed to show its abstract loops; Aubert bought the painting leaning against the desk because the building depicted is around the corner from his childhood home. The walls and trim of the room are painted the same warm, almond-tinted white used in the kitchen and sunroom; the ceiling has a light coat of green glaze, which creates the feeling of being sheltered under a tree.
WALLS AND TRIM: French White, 1093; **CEILING:** Sandy White, 2148-50

The hallway bathroom (right) is painted a pale, watery blue, in a playful fifties pairing with existing bright pink tile. The painted cupboard was given its vivid yellow interior by a friend, who used it for household supplies. "She liked to look at something cheery when she had to clean," the designer says.
WALLS AND TRIM: Stratton Blue, HC-142; **CUPBOARD INTERIOR:** Bold Yellow, 336.

Rooms of one's own

The hallway (above) boasts beautiful pediments above the window and door. Both are picked out in yellow-tinged warm whites, which seem to glow against the taupe walls.
WALLS: Camouflage, 2143-40; **TRIM**: French Canvas, OC-41.

Although the library (opposite) feels like an integral part of the house, it's actually new, with a contemporary tone-on-tone gray palette. The arched bookshelves pay tribute to the home's Carpenter Gothic exterior.
WALLS AND TRIM: Berkshire Beige, AC-2; **BOOKCASE INTERIOR**: Delightful Golden, 2158-30.

WITH FOUR CHILDREN UNDER THE AGE OF twelve in the family, this ornate Carpenter Gothic on the outskirts of Boston is a lively place. Friends, toys, schoolbags, and pets fill the halls, and the communal spaces such as kitchen and family room are a study in controlled, cheerful chaos. Designers Cheryl and Jeffrey Katz were given the challenge of creating a personalized retreat from the general bustle for each member of the household.

In deference to age (and possession of the purse strings), they began with the grown-ups. The couple had requested a library, a peaceful adult haven designed for books, reading, and music, where no television and no toys were allowed. The space includes handsome architectural detail, such as Gothic-style built-in bookshelves, decorative moldings, and a fireplace. The designers built a color palette around the books, taking the parchment, sage, and putty hues right off the bindings. The walls were painted a muted stone-gray color, with low-contrast variations used on trim and woodwork. To inject a dose of visual drama and emphasize the handsome Gothic arches, they painted the interior of the bookshelves a rich pumpkin, then repeated the color in small dashes around the room, including the Roman shade on the window.

For the children's rooms, color was calibrated by personality. The four-year-old girl requested a room full of pinks and mauves, with plenty of space for dress-up and doll storage. The six-year-old boy picked green as his favorite color, so his room was fashioned in shades of bottle, leaf, and lake, with a captain's bed full of storage compartments. The

The emphasis in this family is on reading rather than electronics, so built-in bookshelves and a comfortable curl-up spot are a must in every room. The cozy qualities of the window seat in this little girl's room (right) are enhanced by the slightly darker shade of rose on the walls, which deepens the niche. (Dark colors appear to recede from the eye, and stand up better to the wash of sunlight coming in the window.) The recessed cubbies (below) are a combination of the pink and white wall and trim colors. The pink interior of each square frames objects like a playful shadow box.

WALLS: Spring Blossom, 2172-70.

"KIDS GROW, AND THEIR ROOMS EVOLVE. THE CHALLENGE IS TO FIND COLORS THAT CAN ADAPT TO THEIR CHANGING PERSONALITIES."

—CHERYL KATZ

older boy is a fan of Legos and all things orange; his room boasts a bright orange fireplace surround, with the color repeated on bedding and shades. The other girl got everything on her wish list: pale blues and whites, and a comfy niche for reading and homework.

Finally, a huge basement playroom was created, with a full-length wall of storage for books and games. At its center, like a symbolic hearth, is a generous-size picnic table, painted a fiery carrot color, where the whole family can gather.

An older son's bathroom (above) is also used by guests. The creamy white wainscoting and gray-blue upper walls set a clean, crisp tone that works for everyone.
UPPER WALLS: Grand Rapids, 835;
LOWER WALLS: White Dove, OC-17.

The formal powder room (right) is awash in watery green: A green-tinged slate countertop is backed with green glass tile; the lighting fixture is mounted directly on the mirror. The walls are pale sage, with an even paler sage trim.
WALLS: Silken Pine, 2144-50.
WAINSCOT TRIM: Soft Fern, 2144-40.

The custom-designed bed in this boy's room (left) is like a room within a room, filled with hidden storage and secret spots for stowing treasures. The bed is painted a dark Colonial green, giving it an enveloping quality; the walls are done in a lighter shade of the same color. With all this green above the wheat-colored carpet, the room feels like a little forest.

WALLS: Van Alen Green, HC-120;
BED: Webster Green, HC-130.

In the large playroom (opposite), the walls are white beadboard and the storage shelves are exposed birch. Most of the color comes from the games and toys stowed on the shelves and from the picnic-cum-worktable, which makes a cheery focal point.

PICNIC TABLE: Orange Burst 2015-20.

In children's rooms particularly, color is the easiest thing to change as kids grow and tastes evolve — it's far quicker (and less expensive) to repaint than to replace major furnishings. Try using softer colors on the walls (the soft gray of the library, the silvery green of the boy's room) to make rooms cozy; reserve brighter shades for built-in features, such as bookshelves, window seats, and mantels. Color inspiration can come from unexpected places—books, doll furnishings, toys.

Rhapsody in blues

THIS HISTORIC HOME IN LONG ISLAND'S

Sag Harbor had a long and checkered past before settling down to enjoy its golden years in the care of designer Steven Gambrel. The structure, built around 1810, was originally used as a Methodist meetinghouse: That explains its high ceilings and wide doors, which were atypical for a residence of the time. In 1874, the building was moved a short distance to its current location and turned into a boardinghouse, only to be abandoned toward the end of the 1970s.

When Gambrel purchased the house, it had stood empty for twenty years. Only a few period details remained—the wide board floors, for one—so much was left to the designer's imagination. After immersing himself in the study of the local vernacular, visiting other homes of the period, and poring over plans and sketches, Gambrel began a two-year process of restoring and reinventing the place as a weekend haven.

The house sits directly across the street from the harbor, and the proximity to water makes itself felt in every room. Light bounces off the bay and pours in the windows. The color palette used throughout is based on the shades of the ocean: warm blues played against cool blues; blue-grays and aquamarines fluctuating in the shifting, liquid light.

On the first floor, the colors are layered—the fresh sky blue of the hallway is framed by the sober, chalky blue of the double doors; the aquamarine fabric on an armchair is set against the palest of gray-blues on the living room walls. Upstairs in the bedrooms, the color choices are more autonomous. The master bedroom is robed in a slate-blue gray, and a guest room is built around shades of pale green.

The owner/designer painted the front hall (opposite) twice before hitting upon the right color. The paneled doors are custom-made; the stair rail is based on one he saw in New Orleans.
HALL: Summer Shower, 2135-60;
LIVING ROOM: White Diamond, 2121-60; **TRIM:** White. **DOORS:** Blue Ice, 821.

In the dining room (above), a deep lavender creates the illusion of raised panels on the wall. Adding white to it produced several lighter shades used on the trim and walls.
RAISED PANELS: Lavender Blue, 1438.

"I LOVE A WARM-BASED COLOR AGAINST COOL BLUES." —STEVEN GAMBREL

Every door is painted the same dusty French blue, which serves as a visual connection throughout the house. The deep gray of the master bedroom (left) gives way to the lighter blue-gray of the hall, which in turn morphs into the pale blue-gray of another guest bedroom. The biscuit and camel tones of the linen drapes and bedding provide a warm, earthy note, evoking similar pairings of blue and brown in nature. **BEDROOM WALLS:** Sweatshirt Gray, 2126-40; **.HALL:** Summer Shower, 2135-60; **DOORS:** Swiss Blue, 815; **TRIM:** White.

The pale green guest bedroom (right) was inspired by a trip to Brussels, where the designer fell in love with the heavy, gray-green Belgian linen he turned into curtains, and by the two nineteenth-century gouache landscape panels that now hang in the room.
WALLS: Woodland White, 463; **TRIM:** White.

The serious, slate gray of the dressing room cupboards (below) gives way to a wash of floral pink inside. "I thought of it like the lining of a suit jacket," Gambrel says. "It's fun to have a flash of bright color on the interior—it's a nice, warm way to start the day."
CUPBOARDS: Shadow Gray, 2125-40; Pink Peach 2009-40.

Throughout the house, color is also used to create detail, expressing some visual wit in the process. In the dining room, Gambrel created faux panels and moldings with nothing more than a paintbrush and a few shades of lavender. In the dressing room, the stern gray façades of the built-in drawers hide an interior splash of geranium pink, as surprising and intimate as a glimpse of underclothes.

"When you have such sensational light," Gambrel says of the house, "you have to let it guide your whole approach."

Spanning past and present

THE VERY DEFINITION OF A HISTORIC HOME

is embodied in this classic Greek Revival in upstate New York: From its fluted columns to its mahogany sideboards, it seems steeped in tradition, immune to passing fashions. But when you peek around the corners, you discover an interior that blends respect for the past with a dash of contemporary color sensibility.

The spacious floor plan is much the same as when the house was built in 1825. A formal drawing room, parlor, library, and dining room open off the center hall. In back is a large kitchen, and upstairs, a series of bedrooms. The original wide-board pine floors glow with the burnished caramel color of age.

When designer Margaret Ayers first purchased the house, her intent was to honor its preserved-in-amber quality by choosing a strict palette of historic colors. She researched the Greek Revival period (roughly 1820 to 1840), consulted New York's Cooper Hewitt Museum—and then decided to go with her gut. "I just felt this house was unusual," she says. "It's flooded with light. It could handle stronger color." The drawing room, for example, has floor-to-ceiling windows that face east, west, and south. The rose-pink color Ayers chose for the walls stands up to the wash of sun, at the same time drawing out the auburn tints in the dark-toned, Federal-period furnishings. In a guest bedroom, pale

The drawing room has windows on three sides, so sunlight makes a daylong circuit around the rose-colored walls. The pink, cream, and brown palette is echoed in the Oriental rug, the burgundy sheers and brown velvet drapes, and the burnished tones of the period antiques. The equestrian print and sculpture reflect the owner's passion for the sport.

WALLS: Odessa Pink, HC-59;
TRIM: Ivory White, 925.

In a guest bedroom (above and right), as in the rest of the house, all window frames and woodwork are painted a creamy white, and all mullions are black enamel. "Windows were traditionally painted black to imitate iron," says Ayers. "Now it just makes for an interesting look." The window shades are an antique rose satin that glows almost orange in the afternoon light. The pairing of the red with the green walls intensifies both.
WALLS: Saybrooke Sage, HC-114;
TRIM: Ivory White, 925.

The master bedroom (right) is painted a soft beige with deep pink undertones. The hint of rose draws out the reds of the curtains, rug, and the fabric on the ornate 1830s sofa.
WALLS: Sheraton Beige, HC-57;
TRIM: Ivory White, 925.

The gray bedroom across the hall (below) was inspired by an antique needlepoint floor covering done by a folk-artist relative of the owner. Ayers pulled a shade of gray from the rug, then paired it with the same creamy white used throughout the house.
BEDROOM: Litchfield Gray, HC-78; **HALL:** Lighthouse, 2018-60; **TRIM:** Ivory White, 925.

green walls are paired with rich crimson window shades, giving the room a decidedly modern burst of energy. The pinkish beige in the master bedroom makes a becoming backdrop for antique textiles and a Federal-style sofa, yet it would work equally well in a contemporary setting.

The house is anchored by a characteristic combination of creams and whites in the center hall, and trim is kept to one warm white throughout, to unify the multiple rooms (twelve and counting). "I wanted colors that related to the fabrics and furnishings," says Ayers. "In the bedrooms in particular, that meant being a bit bold."

Black
and blue
all over

Ebony cabinets give a sleek look to the small kitchen (above), more stylish urban bar than utilitarian galley. Mirrored door panels in a small interior hallway (opposite) make the most of what little natural light there is. Glossy black paint and bands of white on the woodwork emphasize the door's clean architectural lines.

WALLS: Faded Denim, 795;
TRIM: Black, Super White.

THE INSPIRATION FOR THE MONOCHROMATIC

color scheme in this tiny New York apartment came right through the bedroom window: Architect Richard Meier's glass-sheathed towers across the street supplied the perfect blue-green shade for the serene interior that designer Miles Redd had in mind. Given the apartment's diminutive size (only 700 square feet), Redd painted the whole space the same color, carrying it up and over the low ceilings. The effect was to blur the small, square proportions and make the walls and ceiling melt together without visual interruption. Since the rooms have little architectural detail, the black-and-white trim colors appear on only the baseboards and doors. To punch up the cool, one-color scheme and keep it from feeling too frosty, the designer used judicious dashes of red—a carefully placed cushion, a warm red-toned wood chair—along with an eclectic mix of mid-century pieces and Chinese antiques.

All the surfaces, including the ceiling, were painted in a high-gloss finish, lending a luminous, shimmery quality to the space. Redd's choice of paint was an unconventional one (because glossy finishes tend to emphasize surface imperfections, they're usually confined to woodwork and trim), but it adds a new layer of textural interest to the apartment and bathes the entire space in a silvery glow. The sheen invites light to linger over the blue-green walls, like sunlight on a still mountain lake—far quieter and more contemplative than you'd guess from the original color chip.

"PEOPLE ARE AFRAID OF BLACK, BUT IT CREATES WONDERFUL CONTRAST AND CRISPNESS IN A ROOM." —MILES REDD

A cheerful striped rug grounds the living room (left and opposite) and keeps the cool color scheme from freezing over; a large, centrally hung mirror draws in and amplifies natural light from the window. Small lamps and sconces play a large part in warming the space and softening the colors by night. (Multiple sources of light are far more flattering than a single overhead fixture.)

The dish-shaped Conran's chair (opposite) adds a note of space-age whimsy as well as serving a practical function: It swivels between the room's two conversation areas. The windows are covered in sheer solar shades to afford privacy without sacrificing light.

WALLS: Faded Denim, 795;
TRIM: Black, Super White.

A single-hue color scheme is a smart choice for a small space with low ceilings. The low contrast look makes the space feel larger, and the ceilings get a lift from the visual continuity with the walls—a particularly good option in rooms with no ceiling moldings. Shiny surfaces add depth and luster, reflecting additional light into the room.

Open to the outdoors

WHEN DESIGNER BENJAMIN NORIEGA-ORTIZ
first saw his client's unprepossessing weekend house on Long Island,
he knew at once that the setting was its strongest feature. The architecture was basic seventies box, with very little detail or character; but
the building was nestled in greenery and adjacent to a large pool, which
supplied dappled shade and watery blue light that poured through the
house's many windows. That blue-green light and the northeastern
coastal location dictated the cool, airy colors that Noriega-Ortiz and
associate Paul Latham used in their makeover.

Since the interior of the house was afflicted with some peculiar
proportions, the designers also chose to use color as a corrective to
create detail and disguise flaws. They covered public rooms in pale
sea-foam greens, blues, and periwinkles to link the indoors to the
water and greenery outside. A portico is draped in fabric to create a
transitional indoor/outdoor room, adding to the building's sense of
transparency and continuity with the landscape. A swath of brilliant
cobalt blue disguises an undistinguished fireplace, making it the
colorful focal point in a featureless room.
Chlorine-blue paint colors connect the
kitchen and dining area to each other and
to the nearby pool. Green garden colors
bloom in the bedrooms, tying the rooms to
the surrounding foliage.

Weather-resistant fabric encloses
the existing portico; the walls
have been painted a gossamer
baby blue. The same shade in
the adjoining entry foyer carries
the color indoors.
WALLS: Blue Allure, 771.

A vibrant cobalt-blue wall in the living room (right) transforms a nondescript fireplace into a stylish statement. There's some visual trickery involved—the designers painted a wider strip on the left than they did on the right, effectively "shifting" the hearth without touching a single brick. "It's a great example of using color to fool the eye," Noriega-Ortiz says. The deep shade also makes a wonderful backdrop for the owners' collections of fifties white glass and milk glass.

WALLS: Fanfare 874;
FIREPLACE: Southern Belle, 819.

The dining area (right) is done in a periwinkle blue, with lavender undertones, that twinkles in the reflected light from the pool. The sea foam green from the adjacent living room is carried over on the ceiling, tying the spaces together.
WALLS: Misty Blue, 820.

The open kitchen (below) is wrapped in the same cool blue as the dining room. Here it provides a clean contrast to the warm-toned maple cabinets, which in turn act as additional accent colors in the room. "I like the mixture of warm and cool," says Noriega-Ortiz. "It's very yin-yang."
WALLS: Misty Blue, 820.

There is a deliberate absence of pattern throughout the house, except for that provided by the play of light. Fabrics and furniture are all solids, to emphasize the sculptural lines. Carrying the concept even further, the furniture in several of the bedrooms was painted to match the walls, transforming the pieces into simple shapes that blend into their surroundings and make the relatively small rooms feel larger.

The little girl who occupies this room (left) was emphatic on one point: no pink. Instead, the walls were painted a deep shade of soothing blue, which calms the colorful jumble of toys and furnishings.
WALLS: Paradise View, 1417.

A guest bedroom (opposite) has large windows that open onto the garden, so the walls were done in a minty apple green to complement the view.
WALLS: Garland Green, 429.

Take the view as your cue. Note the colors and light outside your windows—the blue-gray of the sea, the greens of a luxuriant garden—then bring those shades indoors. Use strong color to create quick architectural fixes, such as disguising boxy proportions, centering an architectural feature, or guiding the eye to a chosen focal point. Remember that cabinetry, wood floors, and furnishings have color of their own. Pair the warm wood tones with cool shades for a clean, modern feel.

Big colors
in a small
package

● ● ● ● ● ● ● ● ● ● ●

In the living room (above), a
nineteenth-century convex mirror
reflects the creamy white of the
walls and ceiling.

WALLS AND TRIM: Mayonnaise,
2152-70.

Coffey replaced the front door of
the house with an inviting entry
hall in back (opposite). The strong
burnt sienna color continues
across the ceiling, transforming the
space into a lacquered red box.

WALLS AND TRIM: Navajo Red,
2171-10.

SEEMINGLY UNREMARKABLE AT FIRST
glance, this Cape Cod is like a birthday present: a big surprise in a
small box. Built in the early 1960s, it had few distinguishing features
and little space (only 1,600 square feet). Yet when designer Birch
Coffey bought it as a weekend retreat, he was taken with the privacy
of the hilly, wooded site and the views it afforded of the Connecticut
countryside. He was also intrigued, oddly enough, by the blandness of
the house itself, which gave him free rein to reshape the structure
according to his own vision.

His first bold move was to enlarge all the windows and do away
with the front door. ("No one in Connecticut uses the front door," says
Coffey, "so I thought, 'Why not have two back doors?'") Then he set
about supplying the character the house lacked, drawing on a palette
of rich, warm, spicy colors to infuse the rooms with drama.

The result flips conventional color advice—stick to light, low-contrast
neutrals to enlarge small rooms—on its head. The smaller, darker
rooms are bathed in opulent color to intensify their snug, welcoming air.
A small entry hall, for example, is painted a deep Chinese red. Coffey's
study is a burnt caramel; his partner's is done in a saffron curry color.
The minute master bedroom is painted a velvety mouse-ear beige.

The larger, lighter public rooms are treated to a buttery white on
walls, ceiling, and trim. The living room draws on the dark tones of
the furnishings and art to supply contrast—the polished-wood tones
of an eighteenth-century French commode, or the crackled varnish of a
seventeenth-century painting.

"COLOR IN SMALL ROOMS IS MORE IMPORTANT THAN IN LARGE ONES, WHERE IT CAN BE OVERWHELMED BY THE ARCHITECTURE. HERE, IT SUPPLIES THE DRAMA."
— BIRCH COFFEY

Butterscotch walls in one study (left) play off the natural wood ceiling and earth tones in the rug. The color is also a nice foil for a collection of eighteenth-century engravings; the paper has faded over the years to a yellowed, tea-stained shade, while the black and gold of the frames lends a crisp, graphic dimension to the room.
WALLS AND TRIM: Golden Tan, 2152-40.

The living room (opposite) is bathed in light from oversize windows. The owner decided to play up the relatively large scale of the room by anchoring the space around dark, overscale furniture and painting walls, ceiling, and trim a pale, creamy yellow that reads as white in this ocher-heavy context.
WALLS AND TRIM: Mayonnaise, 2152-70.

Though the colors throughout the house cover a wide spectrum, they share a warm, earthy, organic quality: If they were woven together as threads in a fabric, the results would be stunning.

"I decided, since the house was small, I'd work from that and make it as cozy and embracing as possible," Coffey says. "And that's just the quality our guests pick up on."

The master bedroom (left) is barely big enough for a bed and two night tables, so it is treated strictly as a sleeping area; soft, somnolent beige walls set a twilight mood. The gray-and-black toile of the curtains and headboard emphasizes the warm gray undertones of the wall color. **WALLS AND TRIM:** Greenbrier Beige, HC-79; **WINDOWS:** Mayonnaise, 2152-70.

Upstairs, doors are treated according to use (opposite below). Closet doors are painted out in the wall color so they blend in. Entrance doors are painted the same color as the trim, making them pop against the walls and creating a kind of visual cue to traffic flow. Baseboards also receive an unusual treatment: The flat surface is black, the rounded top, white, giving the room a snappy frame.
WALLS: Dash of Curry, 2159-10; **TRIM:** Mayonnaise, 2152-70; Black.

This is precisely the sort of conventional house that often gets a conventional color treatment: shades of white to lighten and enlarge small rooms. Instead, the rich hues used here bring the small rooms roaring to life, enhancing their sense of shelter and drama. The cozy dimensions do require discipline: Trim is kept consistent throughout, and the colors are all from the same warm, organic palette. The two-tone baseboards and color-coded doors are novel ideas worth considering.

A second study (above) is wrapped in an appetizing shade of golden brown to compensate for a lack of warm afternoon light. "Quite unintentionally, I chose a lot of food colors," the owner says. "Curry, mayonnaise, caramel—it sounds like a menu." **WALLS**: Dash of Curry, 2159-10. **TRIM**: Mayonnaise, 2152-70.

Neutrals with an attitude

WHEN DESIGNER CAROL BOKUNIEWICZ and her husband first saw their 200-year-old Connecticut farmhouse, it was better suited for livestock than for weekending urbanites. Yet the rural location and ample light appealed. The couple gutted part of the house, creating a clean, spare retreat where unexpected color projects a contemporary sensibility onto a historic screen.

The first floor was reconfigured as an open progression of rooms, with views stretching from the kitchen at one end of the house to the living room at the other. To connect the long sweep of space, floors were stained a uniform white; walls are a series of complex, gray-toned neutrals, punched up with jolts of playful brights and tied together with glossy white trim. Oversize floor-to-ceiling windows flood the living room with light, so the smoky charcoal gray on the walls never seems somber or too dark. The kitchen is a silvery gray-green, which shifts from gray to green to yellow-green as the light changes throughout the day.

But just as the eye settles into this soothing palette, it gets a visual shock that makes the neutrals come alive: A blast of Granny Smith apple green covers one dining room wall, and a powder room explodes in a burst of orange so warm and powerful that it pulsates.

The furnishings add their own quirky mix to the decor. A Lucite coffee table in the living room anchors twin sofas slipcovered in painter's drop cloths. Flea-market pottery congregates above the traditional fireplace. "We didn't want a 'cute' country house," says Bokuniewicz. "We wanted simple, uncluttered rooms with flash points of color. The result doesn't feel slick or urban, just contemporary."

One wall of the dining room (opposite) is done in a crisp green that imparts a youthful energy to the room. "You can make it look elegant, with formal white-on-white table settings, or you can pair it with bright colors for a casual look," says the designer.
WALLS: Chic Lime, 396;
TRIM: White.

The muted shimmer in the kitchen (above) comes from stainless-steel appliances and soft gray-green walls. A George Nelson clock hangs above the stove.
WALLS: Camouflage, 2143-40;
TRIM: White.

The warm pewter gray of the living room (opposite) is balanced by glossy white trim and white furnishings. Against the back wall are Giacometti-inspired lamps in a matte white resin.
WALLS: Shaker Gray, 1594; TRIM: White.

A second-floor guest bedroom (right) is painted a velvety chocolate brown. Abundant natural light helps clarify the color, so the eye can see its depth and complexity. A pony-skin rug echoes the room's color scheme.
WALLS: Chocolate Sundae, 2113-10; TRIM: White.

The powder room (below) is bathed in a blaze of orange-yellow.
WALLS: Bumble Bee Yellow, 2020 10; TRIM: White.

"SMALL BATHS OR HALLS CAN BE GREAT SPOTS FOR STRONG COLOR: THEY ALLOW YOU TO EXPERIENCE THE SHADE IN SMALL DOSES."
— CAROL BOKUNIEWICZ

Quiet riot of color

FAIRLY BURSTING WITH EXUBERANT COLOR, this Manhattan apartment's multihued combinations generate enough energy to light up the block. It's the kind of electric effect that could be shocking if handled carelessly; instead, in the practiced hands of designer Jamie Drake, it delivers an invigorating jolt.

The long, light-filled space was a piano showroom in the last century, though by the time Drake purchased it for his own use, it had been gutted and stripped of any period detail. It still functions as a showroom, however, for the designer's signature love of color and fearless approach to high-impact decor. Just as he has done for celebrity clients around the world, Drake uses powerful, saturated shades that tend to scare off less skillful decorators. His deep magenta foyer, for instance, is not for the faint of heart, yet balanced by a bleached wood floor and white ceiling, the color feels rich and sumptuous rather than overpowering. A chrome-yellow bedroom is another courageous choice, awash in intense citrus shades and spiked with black-and-white animal prints, while a grid of eye-popping cherry reds, lemon yellows, and Caribbean blues forms a raucous mosaic in the powder room.

The success of this space lies in the meticulous placement and balance of color. Throughout the apartment, strong hues are carefully laid out to form a visual progression: the deep magenta of the foyer moves to a lighter fuchsia in the dining room, which

The deep magenta of the entry hall covers everything, including woodwork and trim, to prevent any contrast from altering the color. The fabric on the two upholstered stools provided the inspiration—the designer fell in love with the vibrant shade, then created the entire room around it. **WALLS AND TRIM:** Summer Plum, 2074-20.

The insouciant pink of the dining area (left) makes a lively background for art by day (painting by Chuck Close) and creates a flattering, rosy light by night. **WALLS**: Exotic Fuchsia, 2074-50; Point Beach, 1136; **TRIM**: Ivory White, 925.

The same pink is carried over into the living room (opposite and below), where it pops up on upholstery and lampshades, though here it is calmed by warm beige walls and curtains. This is the only area where the designer used color on the ceiling—he painted it a pale blue-gray to give it more height—then added a large, stylized molding. Despite the vivacious dashes of color, the room feels tranquil and composed. **WALLS**: Point Beach, 1136; **TRIM**: White Blush, 904; **CEILING**: Crystal Blue, 2051-70.

fades to pinkish beige in the living room. The result is a whole that is more harmonious than its individual parts, the striking tones mixing and matching to create a formal, almost sartorial elegance. Says Drake of his approach, "I'm not looking to create somnambulant interiors. I want to walk into a room and feel invigorated."

"COLOR IN TREMENDOUS QUANTITY CAN HAVE A RESTFUL EFFECT. YOU END UP FOCUSING LESS ON THE COLOR AND MORE ON TEXTURE."

—JAMIE DRAKE

The powder room (top left) is a tongue-in-cheek tribute to the designer's reputation as a colorful character. The upper walls were masked off into squares that mirrored the tiles below, then painted in a crazy quilt of cheerful hues.

The master bedroom (right) is divided from the rest of the space by a pivoting door, enameled an intense yellow. The walls are an acidic yellow, inspired by an Indian silk that became the long, flowing bedroom curtains. "For a person who loves color, yellow was never a favorite, but I wanted something provocative and piquant," says Drake. The bathroom wall (bottom left) is done in sponged graphite gray.

WALLS AND TRIM: Dalila, 319; Yellow Finch, 2024-40;
BATHROOM WALL: Ashland Slate, 1608.

Drake's trademark technique is to choose strong colors, then spike them with some unexpected shade from the opposite side of the color wheel: magenta paired with jade green, tangerine with bright blue. Floors are bleached a uniform platinum blonde to allow the color fields to float above them. Saturated jewel tones are used at their most intense, so colors sparkle.

A Tiffany gift box

All the furniture in the main living area (opposite) is slipcovered in white cotton duck and punched up with scattered black-and-white accessories, including zebra-stripe pillows. Aside from these animal patterns, the only other accent colors come from the art and objects on the walls. Floor-to-ceiling windows flood the room with light, softening the intense background. In the small triangular entry hall (above), the bright blue used throughout the apartment darkens and intensifies.
WALLS: Tropicana Cabana, 2048-50; **TRIM:** White; **CEILING:** Crystal Blue, 2051-70.

THE OWNER OF THIS LIGHT-FILLED URBAN loft wanted a high-impact look on a low-impact budget. She turned to interior designer Miles Redd, whose love of bright color and broad streak of whimsy had served her well in previous homes. Together, they created a cool, breezy aesthetic packed with visual wit.

The bold blue that covers all the walls could be pure Holly Golightly. The designer pulled it right off the side of a Tiffany's box, then had his paint dealer match the shade to the noted jeweler's signature packaging. Floors and trim are painted a high-gloss white with cool ocean undertones, and the ceiling is painted a paler shade of glossy sky blue. The space is large and the ceilings high enough to carry the punch of such a powerful color, and the intense expanse of blue makes a surprisingly strong backdrop for the owner's eclectic art collection.

So many glossy surfaces contribute to the watery, Caribbean feel of the space, inspired by the owner's family home in Antigua. Crisp white slipcovers and black-and-white accents on fabrics and floor coverings pop out against the bright background, adding a bit of contrast and pattern to an essentially one-color environment. In a sleight of hand, the painted white floor makes the furniture seem to float like clouds in a blue sky.

"This is definitely a cooler look," says Redd, "but good lighting works to warm it up. And high gloss helps—at night, the reflection gives you a luminosity and warmth you wouldn't have in a flat color."

In a corner of the living area (left), the plain white slipcover takes on a blue tinge thanks to its proximity to the blue walls. The bubble lamp is made of mercury glass. The room's sheer striped curtains (bottom left) reach from floor to ceiling, emphasizing the verticality of the room. The play of light on the beamed ceiling—painted a uniform pale blue—gives it a coffered look.
WALLS: Tropicana Cabana, 2048-50; **TRIM:** White; **CEILING:** Crystal Blue, 2051-70.

The bedroom niche (opposite) is set off by louvered screens. A wall of closets behind the bed is painted with pale blue squares in the same color as the ceiling to break up the boxy doors.
WALLS: Tropicana Cabana, 2048-50; **TRIM:** White; **CEILING AND DOOR PANELS:** Crystal Blue, 2051-70.

The lesson in this playful home is that there is no such thing as too bold in a big, bright space. Such intense color could be overpowering in a small, dark room, but here, washed by sun and diluted by high ceilings, it feels airy and refreshing.

This pairing of cool blue with equally cool trim colors (minty whites with blue and green undertones) probably plays best in a warm room with a southern or western exposure.

If you do choose blue, remember that lavender blues feel more feminine, navies more masculine. Mid-tones and green blues usually read as gender neutral.

Shades of urban cool

The library walls (above and opposite) are a blue deep enough to deprive you of oxygen. Surprisingly, the super high-gloss finish reflects so much light that the room seems to shimmer despite the dark shade. Tall, white-trimmed doorways pull the eye to the lighter space beyond, while deep velvets and luxurious textures soften the shiny, hard surfaces. A collection of sixties and seventies art glass adds extra sparkle to a corner near the window.

WALLS: Old Glory, 811; **TRIM:** White; **DOORS:** Jet Black, 2120-10. 2120-10.

CAN A GLOOMY WARREN OF OFFICES become a sleek urban home? This sophisticated Park Avenue apartment in a 1920s building was created almost entirely from scratch, once the current owners saw the potential in the jumble of rooms, and hired designer Steven Gambrel to help them reclaim the space.

The challenge was to impose a graceful residential flow on the oddly configured living area and deliver enough light to the dark interior rooms. Gambrel's approach was based on the European concept of *enfilade*: He gutted the space, then positioned the rooms so that they open onto each other rather than onto a hallway, thus maximizing the size and spacious feel of the apartment.

Because of the long sight lines and open floor plan, it was particularly important to create an integrated color palette. Gambrel chose a suave and stylish assortment of deep blues, steels, and platinums, with highly polished and reflective surfaces bouncing light back into the rooms. The library, for example, is done in a high-gloss navy so deep that it looks black, especially when paired with the bright white trim. Wide, eight-foot-high doors open onto a living room painted a pale steely shade. The kitchen is done in more platinum and blue-gray tones, balanced, as in the rest of the house, by super-white ceilings and trim.

Black is a common thread in the 2,800-square-foot space: The wood floors are ebonized, and oversize doors throughout are painted a shiny black to attract and reflect the scarce light. "The backgrounds and surfaces were intended to be very icy, very polished, very urbane," says Gambrel. "You can add warmth through fabrics and furnishings."

The pale pewter tones of the living room (left) are picked up in the warm champagne-colored satin of the chair; even the fabric reflects light, bouncing it into the darker library beyond. The trim around the fireplace is a clean piece of modernist millwork. "We wanted a clean, spare version of a classic Park Avenue prewar apartment," says the designer. A flat-screen plasma television is sunk into the wall above the fireplace.

WALLS: White Diamonds, 2121-60; **TRIM:** White; **DOORS:** Jet Black, 2120-10.

In the long, rectangular kitchen (left), the eating area is at one end, the appliances at the other. The apartment's cool, blue-gray palette continues here, but it is warmed by the wood tones from the chairs and the buttery leather of the built-in banquette.
WALLS: White Diamonds, 2121-60. **TRIM:** White; **CABINETS:** Marilyn's Dress, 2125-60.

"IN A LIGHT-DEPRIVED SPACE, EVERY SURFACE SHOULD BE WORKING TO REFLECT AND REFRACT LIGHT."
—STEVEN GAMBREL

practical matters

For homeowners who plan to do their own painting, here are some practical guidelines and tips on how to achieve smooth, professional results that will show off the colors to their best advantage

Before you begin

Perhaps most important, choose good-quality rollers and brushes. Look for brushes with long, dense, and "flagged" (rather than square-cut) bristles, which look like the split ends of hair. This is no time to economize: A good set of brushes, if cleaned and stored correctly, will deliver a superior paint finish and last for years. Inferior brushes give poor results and fall apart quickly.

Temperature

The ideal temperature for interior painting is 70°F with adequate ventilation (although most paints can be used at temperatures as low as 50°F). At around 70°F, and about 50 percent humidity, paint will dry properly and glide on easily. In some climates, that may mean postponing a job until you hit a stretch of mild weather; the temperature could drop well below 70°F if you open windows on a frigid day in February.

Have on hand:

- Paint—enough to have some left over for future touch-ups
- Roller, with an extension handle for ceilings, and a tray. Disposable tray inserts save cleanup time.
- Brushes. A two-inch angled sash brush and a three-inch trim brush should cover all your needs. Choose nylon bristles for latex paint and natural bristles for oil.
- Stepladder. Wobbly chairs and stools are trouble.
- Drop cloths. Plastic is good for protecting furniture but slippery underfoot. Canvas is safer, absorbs spills, and will last forever.
- Clean rags. You can never have enough.
- Single-edge razor blades
- Low-tack painter's tape, available at any paint store. Do not use masking tape—it can pull the paint off the walls.
- Bucket and sponge
- Mineral spirits for cleanup when using oil paints. Also called paint thinner or solvent.
- Spackling compound
- Putty knives
- Sanding block
- Screwdriver
- Can opener
- Mixing sticks
- Trim guard or rigid cardboard, for painting baseboards and moldings.

Clearing the space

Remove everything you can from the room or area to be painted—furniture, lamps, pictures, window treatments, rugs. If something is too big or bulky, move it to the center of the room and cover it with a plastic drop cloth. Lay a heavy canvas drop cloth on the floor where you'll be painting. Make sure you have a perfectly flat surface for your paint cans and other equipment.

Preparing surfaces

This is probably the most time-consuming and least enjoyable part of painting, but it's also the step that pays off most in the end. A clean, dry, well-primed surface makes for a long-lasting paint job, and a smooth, uniform finish makes colors look their best. It saves work in the long run—do it once, do it right, and you won't have to do it again for a long time.

• If the walls are dirty, greasy, or food stained (above a kitchen stove, for example), wash with a sponge and soapy water, then rinse and allow to dry. Scrape off loose or flaking paint with a putty knife, then sand smooth. Fill small cracks or holes with spackling compound; large holes may need a second application. When dry, sand smooth; use a dust mask to avoid breathing any particles.

• Remove all switch plates and wash them off. If you plan to paint them, do it before reinstalling them and allow to dry first. If you're going to use a glossy finish on trim, sand the plates slightly to dull the surface, then wipe them down with a tack cloth.

• Spot-prime tough stains or patched spots with a specialty primer to prevent bleeding through the finish coat. (See "Prime Time" on page 137 for further guidelines on priming.

Painting

Start with the ceiling; then do the walls, working from top to bottom. Always work quickly enough to maintain a "wet edge" between sections. Plan the job so you can complete the ceiling (or the walls) without interruption. Leave the trim for last.

Ceilings

1. Loosen the collars of all hanging light fixtures, drop them a few inches away from the ceiling, then wrap with newspaper to protect from splatters.

Plan ahead

• To keep colors uniform, don't wait till you're down to the end of one can before opening another. When a can is three-quarters empty, stir up a new gallon and add it to the open one. Pour the paint back and forth a few times to ensure color uniformity and to eliminate any streaks or spots.

• Remove all switch-plate covers when painting a room; before replacing them, put a dab of each new color on the back, and write the color name and number in permanent marker next to it. When you repaint or touch up, you'll have a handy record of which colors were used.

Open windows and doors while you work, to allow full access to all surfaces. Tackle them first thing in the morning so they'll be dry enough to close at night without sticking or pulling off the new paint. If you are using oil-based paint and need to take an overnight break between coats, wrap brushes and rollers in plastic and put them in the freezer. Take them out the next morning, allow them to warm, and you're ready to resume work. Don't try this with latex, as water-based paints will freeze.

2. Working your way around the perimeter of the ceiling, paint a three-inch strip along the wall/ceiling line with a brush (this is called "cutting in").

3. Attach the extension handle to your roller and begin to roll paint onto a four-foot section of ceiling; the roller should be saturated with paint, but not dripping. After you've applied the paint in one direction, roll lightly, without refilling the roller, in a cross direction to eliminate roller marks. As you paint a second area, again lightly roll in a cross direction toward the first area, tapering off into the previous work to blend the two sections together. Work

quickly to maintain a "wet edge" between sections.

Walls

1. Start in a corner of the room. Using a brush, paint a vertical strip that covers one side of the corner, then paint a horizontal strip about six feet long where the wall meets the ceiling (or the crown molding). With a brush and edge guard, paint another six-foot strip where the wall meets the baseboard, carpet, or floor.

2. Load the roller with paint and fill in the wall section between the stripes. Work quickly enough to maintain a wet edge between the painted stripes and the rolled middle so they blend smoothly.

You can roll in an M or W pattern, or roll a vertical section and then go over it horizontally with the dry roller as you did on the ceiling.

3. Move along the wall, continuing to paint the strips at top and bottom and then filling in the middle. Overlap each new section with the previously painted section so there is no visible edge. Plan to paint an entire wall without taking a break, so the edges don't have time to dry.

Doors

Try to start this project first thing in the morning so they'll be dry enough to close by evening.

• If you're using an oil-based paint, you may need to remove the door entirely and lay it flat on sawhorses. This allows the paint time to dry and prevents sagging or visible drips. To remove doors, simply tap the bottom end cap off the hinge, then tap each pin up and out of its hinge with a hammer and screwdriver. Loosen the collar around the doorknob, or mask it off carefully with tape.

Prime time

Priming covers stains, seals the surface, prolongs the wet edge as you paint the finish coat, and ensures a uniform color and finish.

You should prime:

- All untreated and unpainted surfaces.
- When using a deep color. Ask your paint dealer to tint the primer to a lighter version of the top coat color.
- When going from a dark to a light color, for better coverage.
- When a wall has been painted so many times that the latex layers become absorbent; priming will reseal the surface.
- When trying to cover crayon marks or other stains that could "bleed" through the finish coat.

You don't have to prime:

- When repainting relatively new walls in a similar color.
- When painting trim, windows, and doors that have a semi-gloss coat in good condition.

- With latex paint, you probably don't need to remove the doors; just protect the handles with plastic bags and mask off the collars with tape.
- Prop the door open so the edges are accessible and you can work comfortably. Paint panels first, then the framework (horizontal pieces first, then the verticals). If the door is flush, begin at the top and work down in long, vertical strokes. Keep the brush loaded with paint and work quickly, always brushing down into the wet areas. Coat all four door edges, keeping a damp rag handy in case paint runs onto the reverse side.

Windows

As with doors, start this project as early in the day as possible so they'll be dry enough to close by evening.

1. Unscrew and remove the sash lock. Lower the upper part of the window and raise the lower part so the sash is clear of the sill.

2. Paint the sash, then the rails. Raise the upper part of the window and repeat the process.

3. To complete the window, coat the rails, frame and sill. Never paint the sash tracks, to avoid sticky window mechanisms.

4. To paint window mullions, either mask off the glass with painter's tape (remove as soon as you're finished or the tape may stick) or paint directly along the glass and use a razor blade to scrape off any smears or

Cover-ups

Radiators, exposed pipes, clumsy cables—almost any defect can be disguised with a few coats of paint. Blend eyesores into the background with same-color wall paint; remember to prime any unpainted surface first. Use accent colors to pick out only those features you want to emphasize, such as windows, moldings, and doors.

spatters when dry. Remember to leave the window slightly open until the paint is completely dry.

Trim

Using the edge of the brush, carefully coat the edge of the trim nearest the wall, then paint the facing. If you don't trust yourself to paint freehand, mask off the wall with low-tack painter's tape. (Remove the tape as soon as you're finished painting.) With door trim, extend the color inside the doorway to include the inner face of the frame, the part covered by the door when closed.

Baseboard and molding

Protect your floor or carpeting with an edge guard or a rigid piece of cardboard and painter's tape. Tape off the floor surface, then hold the trim guard or cardboard below the brush as you paint. Be sure to wipe off the guard before painting each new section. Use the same procedure for painting a crown molding: Tape off the

ceiling and walls, and use the trim guard, wiping it thoroughly each time you move to an adjacent section.

Cleanup

For oil-based paints, work mineral spirits into the brush bristles, squeeze out the liquid, and repeat until paint is gone. Rinse in solvent and let dry. Roller covers are not worth the trouble of cleaning with solvent—allow to dry and dispose of properly. For latex paints, simply work warm soapy water through brushes and roller covers, rinse, wring out excess liquid, and hang to dry.

Storage

Leftover paint can last for years with proper storage.

• Cover the opening of the can with plastic wrap and replace the lid, tapping it down firmly with a rubber mallet so it is secure. Store the can upside down; this creates a tight seal, keeping the paint fresh for future touch-ups or projects and ensuring that any film or crust that forms will

Brushes and rollers

- Hairs and fibers can ruin a fresh coat of paint. To prevent brush bristles or roller fibers from shedding and sticking, flex all new brushes over your hand a few times before painting so any loose bristles will fall out.

- Comb through older brushes with a special brush comb before use.

- Wrap rollers in masking tape, then pull off to remove loose fibers.

- To save an expensive brush that has dried stiff and out of shape, just dip it in boiling water, comb it straight, and hang it up to dry.

- If you're painting trim with an oil-based paint or alkyd enamel, use a good-quality natural-bristle brush. Use a synthetic-blend nylon trim brush with latex paint.

- For best results and paint adhesion, choose the correct roller cover for the surface you're painting. Choose short-napped, smooth covers for smoother surfaces such as drywall, and longer-napped covers for rougher surfaces such as textured plaster or paneling. Reserve the longest, fuzzy-napped covers for the roughest surfaces, such as brick or stucco.

end up on the bottom when you reopen the can. Remember to label the can with the date and room where the paint was used.

• Always store brushes flat on their sides, rolled in newspaper, or hung on a hook. If they're kept head down (in a bucket, for example), the bristles will become splayed and loose.

Paint types

Primer

The first coat for any unpainted or untreated surface, it seals off the surface and promotes better paint adhesion. For interior painting, oil and latex primers can be used almost interchangeably. If you use a latex primer, however, you must cover it with a latex paint. If you use an oil-based primer, you can use either latex or oil paint as a top coat. There is also a wide variety of primers and sealants available for any special surface (metal, stucco, etc.); consult your local paint dealer.

Latex paint

The most popular finish for nearly all interior needs. Because it is water-based, latex paint is easy to apply and quick to dry and clean up with soap and water.

Solvent-based oil paint

Slower to dry and tougher to clean up, oil paint is used less frequently in home interiors. High-gloss versions are sometimes used on doors and trim because of their smooth, mirror-like finish, free of visible brush strokes.

Latex floor enamel

Specially formulated to stand up to foot traffic, floor enamels are durable, washable with soaps and detergent, and deliver a smooth, uniform appearance.

Clear wood finish

Sometimes used to give a clear protective coat to painted floors; available in latex and oil. New latex versions offer improved durability, without the yellowing that can sometimes occur with oil-based varieties.

Paint finishes

Both oil and latex paints come in a variety of sheens, from no shine at all to highly reflective. The relative degree of shine affects durability—generally, the higher the gloss, the more long-lasting the finish—but there is also an aesthetic component: A lustrous, light-reflecting finish

• Tape is an essential part of your painter's toolbox. Despite the name, never use masking tape to mask anything. If you need to protect a surface from wet paint, use low-tack painter's tape, which will pull off easily without damaging the underlying finish. Masking tape can pull paint right off the wall, and take some of the Sheetrock or plaster with it.

• Always remove tape as soon as you're done painting, when the surface is still wet.

has a very different look from that of a velvety matte surface.

Flat

A flat, no-shine finish that absorbs light rather than reflecting it, so it tends to mask surface imperfections and irregularities. It's the most common choice for ceilings. It can be used on walls, though it won't stand up to stains or washing—not a good choice in high-traffic areas.

Matte

Although this stylish no-shine alternative to flat paint on walls has little to no sheen, some of the newer formulas are as washable as a semigloss. They're perfect for areas where you want a washable flat finish.

Eggshell

This finish, and related finishes sometimes called pearl or satin, has a slight, satiny sheen, making it more resistant to stains and more amenable to washing than flat paint. A particularly popular finish on walls.

Semigloss

Shiny without looking wet, this is the finish of choice for trim, doors, and windows. The higher gloss makes it more resistant to stains, and it can stand up to frequent washing (important for touchable areas such as banisters, door frames, cupboards, etc.). Semigloss is probably the most common finish for interior trim.

High-gloss

The shiniest finish available, usually reserved for picking out trim or emphasizing doors. It dries to a hard, mirrorlike sheen, and is extremely durable. For the glossiest finish, some painters choose oil-based paints over latex because they dry more slowly, giving brush marks time to disappear completely.

An ounce of prevention

- Always set open paint cans and roller trays flat on a level patch of floor; make sure drop cloths are smooth and even.

- Despite drop cloths and trim guards, spills and spatters happen. The most important thing is to clean up immediately, before paint dries. Use mineral spirits for oil-paint spills and soapy water for latex. Keep a damp rag with you at all times (a textured terry washcloth works well) and wipe off latex smears as they occur.

- With the exception of flat finishes or ceiling paint, most painted surfaces are washable, but this simple kitchen tip can make cleaning a painted wall or door even easier: Add a drop of dishwashing liquid to the water to prevent streaking. Just as dish soap keeps suds from drying in streaks on your glassware, it will keep streaky sponge marks from drying on walls or trim.

Lead Paint Safety
Lead compounds were used in paints for hundreds of years and were quite common up to the first half of the twentieth century. In 1978, the federal government prohibited the use of lead in the manufacture of architectural coatings.

Old paint that is adhering well and isn't cracking, flaking, or chalking does not present a hazard even if it contains lead. However, if old paint is sanded, scraped, or otherwise disturbed, dust is generated, which may pose a lead hazard. Any work on homes built prior to 1978 requires special precautions to protect both the occupants and workers. Dust or fumes containing lead can cause serious injury and are especially dangerous to children and pregnant women.

Controlling exposure to lead or other hazardous substances requires the use of proper protective equipment, such as a properly fitted respirator (NIOSH approved), and proper work practices, including containment of dust and fumes and careful cleanup of the work area.

For additional information, contact the USEPA Lead Information Hotline at 1-800-424-LEAD or www.epa.gov/lead, or visit your local independent paint retailer.

Paint Disposal
Disposal of any liquid paint is a problem for sanitation collectors and for the landfill, and most municipalities have strict rules against it. Empty paint cans are no problem—just let them dry in the air for a few days, then dispose of them along with your trash. Better yet, take advantage of recycling programs for steel and plastic in your community. Cans containing a small amount of paint can be left to dry out, or the paint can be poured into a cardboard box containing shredded paper or cat litter and left to dry. Once dry, the whole container can be disposed of with your trash. Cans containing too much paint to dry efficiently should be sealed and stored until your next household hazardous waste collection day, which most municipalities hold once or twice a year. However, consider retaining enough paint for touch-ups or donating quantities of leftover paint to a community-based organization that may need it.

Rags and tools soaked in oil paint, thinner, or stain can spontaneously ignite under certain conditions, so they present a special hazard. They should be thoroughly dried before they are put in the trash or immersed in water until they can be disposed of safely.

General Safety Note
Always wear proper protective clothing, and follow the manufacturer's recommendations for the correct use and handling of equipment, paints, stains, and all other materials mentioned in this book.

For additional product and application information, please call Benjamin Moore Customer Service at 1-800-6-PAINT-6 or visit www.benjaminmoore.com.

Photography Credits

Gordon Beall pages 16–17, 55–57.

John Bessler pages 1, 4, 10, 12 (top and bottom), 14, 15, 19, 21, 22 (bottom), 29, 30, 37, 38, 40, 64–75, 80–85, 96–103, 110–129, 144.

Hornick/Rivlin pages 12 (middle), 86–91.

Property of Benjamin Moore pages 26, 54, 58, 59.

Tim Street-Porter pages 2–3, 7–9, 22 (top), 33, 34, 48–53, 60–63, 92–95, 104–109, 130.

Vicente Wolf pages 42–47.

Acknowledgments

Smallwood & Stewart wish to thank the architects, designers, and homeowners who allowed us to photograph the properties featured in this book and who gave so generously of their time in explaining their approaches to color. Thanks also to Bruce Glickman and Wilson Henley of Duane, New York, and to Bruce Shostak, all of whom provided invaluable help in the early stages of the book.

Design Credits

The room on page 1 was designed by Birch Coffey; pages 2–3, Benjamin Noriega-Ortiz; page 4, Jamie Drake; page 7, Steven Gambrel; page 8, Michael Bruno; page 10, Margaret Ayers; pages 16–17, Darryl Carter; page 144, Jamie Drake.

Designer Directory

LOUIS AUBERT, ASID
39 Neron Place
New Orleans, LA 70118
(504) 861-0968

MARGARET C. AYERS &
ASSOCIATES
Box 178
Claverack, NY 12513
(518) 851-6060
mcarscf@aol.com

CAROL BOKUNIEWICZ
Carol Bokuniewicz Design
73 Spring Street
New York, NY 10012
(212) 941-1350

MICHAEL BRUNO
950 Third Avenue
New York, NY 10022
(212) 994-7543
www.1stdibs.com

DARRYL CARTER
Darryl Carter Inc.
2342 Massachusetts Avenue
Washington, D.C., N.W. 20008
(202) 234-5926
www.darrylcarter.com

BIRCH COFFEY
Birchfield Studio, LTD.
52 Longpond Road
PO Box 1353
Lakeville, CT 06039
(860) 435-8016

JAMIE DRAKE
Drake Design Associates
315 East 62nd Street
New York, NY 10021
(212) 754-3099

STEVEN GAMBREL
270 Lafayette Street
Suite 805
New York, NY 10012
(212) 925-3380

C&J KATZ STUDIO
60 K Street
South Boston, MA 02127
(617) 464-0330

BENJAMIN NORIEGA-ORTIZ
Benjamin Noriega-Ortiz LLC
75 Spring Street, 6th floor
New York, NY 10012
(212) 343-9709
www.BNOdesign.com

MILES REDD
77 Bleecker Street
Suite C111
New York, NY 10012
(212) 674-0902
www.milesredd.com

VICENTE WOLF
Vicente Wolf Associates
333 West 39th Street
10th Floor
New York, NY 10018
(212) 465-0590
www.vicentewolfassociates.com